Informalize!

ETH Zurich
Werk 11

Informalize!

Essays on the Political Economy of Urban Form

Vol. 1

Edited by
Marc Angélil & Rainer Hehl

RUBY PRESS

WERK 11: A Laboratory for Contemporary Urban Design and Research

The present collection of essays marks the beginning of a series of contributions on contemporary urban theory that will be presented and discussed
within the context of a new design and research center at the ETH Zurich—
WERK 11.

Established in a former factory building as an outpost of the Department of
Architecture, WERK 11 is a laboratory and center for expertise that brings
together the various fields that have an impact on today's urban conditions.
It provides open ateliers, workshops, and seminar and lecture spaces join-
ing the ETH professorships of Prof. Alfredo Brillembourg and Prof. Hubert
Klumpner, Prof. Kees Christiaanse, Prof. Günther Vogt, Prof. Christophe Girot,
Prof. Dr. Christian Schmid, and Prof. Dr. Marc Angélil. As a combination of a
research center, design studio, and event space, it encourages a dialogue
between theory and practice and establishes networks between the academic
field and the multiple actors involved in the production of the city. By thinking
architecture, sociology, landscape and urban design beyond their disciplinary
boundaries, WERK 11 hopes to both understand and shape existing and future
urban and rural environments, whether in the immediate context of the Swiss
agglomeration or in the megacities of the Global South.

Among the ETH professorships that operate within the context of WERK 11,
the Chair of Prof. Dr. Marc Angélil engages with contemporary urban research,
as well as topics on the edge of the discipline, including urban poverty,
ageing demographics, and large-scale retail logistics. The Chair's research
seminar and lecture series, Urban Mutations on the Edge (UME), investigates
provocative ideas and innovative projects that deal with a wide range of
topics. Set against more traditional notions of architecture and urban
design, this interdisciplinary approach asks what one branch of knowledge
can bring to the other.

The first issue in the Essays on the Political Economy of Urban Form
series addresses the topic of informality with a selection of contributions
to the UME lecture series by Tom Avermaete, Fran Tonkiss, Milica Topalović,
and Ananya Roy.

Contents:

UME Research:
ETH Zurich

In Search of
the Determinants
of Urban Form

An Introduction
by Rainer Hehl

"A new science called 'political economy' and, at the same time, a characteristic form of governmental intervention, that is, intervention in the field of economy and population, will be brought into being by reference to this continuous and multiple network of relationships between the population, the territory and wealth. In short, the transition in the eighteenth century from a regime dominated by structures of sovereignty to a regime dominated by techniques of government revolves around population, and consequently around the birth of political economy."[1]

- Michel Foucault

If we take Michel Foucault's definition of the political economy as both a science and technique used by governments to structure populations, territories, and wealth, then the study of urban form as a physical manifestation of the political economy can reveal the social, economic, and political implications embedded in the city. This becomes all the more apparent as urban planners lose control of urban development to the dynamics of ad-

1 Michel Foucault, *Security, Territory, Population: Lectures at the Collège de France, 1977-1978* (Basingstoke: Palgrave Macmillan Ltd., 2007), 206.

vanced capitalism: the fundamentalism of neoliberal politics, the domination of financial capital, and the privatization of public space. Whether we look at the empty, sprawling suburbs left behind by the U.S. subprime mortgage crisis or the slums that continue to increase in size and number, the crisis of the human habitat clearly reflects the failure of our current urban economy to serve the basic needs of a constantly growing population. While we can trace the crisis of the prevailing system in the political and economic implications of contemporary space, the city of today and tomorrow is increasingly shaped by agencies, negotiation processes, and power structures outside our traditional understanding of urban development. In turn, this multiplicity of urban forms also marks the materialization of new social, economic, and cultural orders.

With the curiosity to cross disciplinary boundaries, this first volume of contributions from the UME lecture series at the ETH, Zurich, explores the topic of urban informality. Within the context of African urban studies, the International Labor Organization (ILO) first introduced the term "informality" in a 1972 report on the informal sector in Nairobi. The ILO report codified a language to describe informal settlements that continues to be used by scholars up to this day. According to the report, urban informality applies to areas where the informal sector has a base, services are poor or non-existent, residents are invisible to legal frameworks, and harassment by authorities is commonplace.[2] The characteristics of the activities of the informal sector, including "ease of entry, reliance on indigenous resources, family ownership of enterprises, labor-intensive and adapted technology, skills outside the formal school system, and

2 ILO, *Employment, Incomes and Equality: A Strategy for Increasing Productive Employment in Kenya* (Geneva: ILO, 1972), 6.

unregulated and competitive markets," are evaluated against what are often large-scale and high-tech formal systems of laws and regulations.[3]

While some informal environments still meet all of these qualifications, not all do; it is therefore virtually impossible to establish a clear definition of urban informality. In part, this is because it manifests itself today in many different ways. But it is also because informal and formal systems are increasingly connected and interdependent. Long ascribed to the infamous urban growth of the Global South, urban informality can in fact no longer be understood as a shadow world excluded from capitalist markets and public welfare systems. In the words of Ananya Roy and Nezar AlSayyad, "urban informality does not simply consist of the activities of the poor, or a particular status of labor, or marginality. Rather, it is an organizing

3 ILO, *Employment, Incomes and Equality.*

logic which emerges under a paradigm of liberalization."[4] Whether we then interpret urban informality as "liberalization from below" or disqualify it as a threat to the very project of the city and a desperate attempt to access the free-market economy, urban informality is and has to be recognized as a dominant mode of urban production.[5]

To reflect the many manifestations of urban informality, this publication collects four articles that offer unique and international insights into the phenomenon. In the first article, "Accommodating the Afropolis," Tom Avermaete traces the career of Michel Ecochard and the development of the transnational urban planning expert. As the chief urban planner in Morocco during the forties and the fifties,

4 Ananya Roy and Nezar AlSayyad, *Urban Informality: Transnational Perspectives from the Middle East, Latin America and South Asia* (Lanham: Lexington Books, 2004), 26.
5 The projection that in about twenty years, half of the world's urban population will live in self-built structures erected beyond official planning and state control illustrates the magnitude of an urban reality that might be far more complex, diverse, and unexplored than the type of cities that we have focused on so far. See United Nations Human Settlements Programme, *The Challenge of Slums* (Nairobi: UN-Habitat, 2003).

Ecochard developed strategies for urban development that for the first time recognized informal building practices and traditional customs and combined them with the formal approach of the functionalist planning of the time. To this day, the gridded carpet settlements introduced by Ecochard still define the overgrown urban fabric of Casablanca. Intentionally or not, the democratization of space has occurred not by any act of the Moroccan government, but by the daily appropriation of *la Trame Ecochard* by the Moroccan people.

The challenge that Ecochard's practice raises against the dichotomy of the informal and formal is furthered by Fran Tonkiss, who emphasizes the ambiguity and flexibility of what we describe as informal. In her article, "Informality and Its Discontents," the term is discussed not through any prevailing discourse, but through the very contradictions that define it: organic settlements versus slums, self-help versus abandonment, social capital versus racketeering, temporary use versus insecurity, looseness versus disorder, and, finally, commonalty versus invasive publicness. After unraveling the many inconsistencies that allow informality to translate between the developed and developing world, what remains is the ability of the ordinary inhabitant to enact and influence the making and remaking of our cities.

Surprisingly efficient, stable, and "normal," the total informalism of Belgrade, Serbia, is a perfect example of informality's contradictions. In "Brick and Gold," Milica Topalović writes that Belgrade did not gradually informalize over time; instead, informal construction was and remains both the standard and the basis for post-factum legislation and planning in Belgrade. In arguing the efficiency and stability of these informal negotiations and ad hoc planning practices, Topalović shows

how urban informality has appropri-
ated urban elements that are constitutive to the construction of normality,
such as infrastructure, street names,
and public spaces. The legalization
of illegally occupied agricultural land,
coupled with the privatization of the
city's assets, created a new model of
the suburb, argues Topalović: Oriented
towards the city center, these informal
neighborhoods appear as successful
social projects where Belgrade's Wild
Rich, farmers, and paupers all share
the same space.

Investigating subaltern spaces,
Ananya Roy takes us to the most
iconic and common itinerary through
which the mega-city is recognized and
stereotyped: the Third World slum.
With Dharavi in India as a case study,
the protests against *Slumdog Millionaire* and the stigma of underdevelopment provide a starting point for a
two-pronged revision of the subaltern.
The first revision challenges the post-

colonial treatment of the subaltern as a space defined by difference. Looking at four emergent urban phenomena caused by transformations in the Global South, Roy sees the subaltern as an agent of change and subaltern urbanism as a space defined by vibrant entrepreneurial urbanism and political agency. While marking the limits of ethnographic and archival recognition, Roy's analysis of the concept of the subaltern goes even further. For Roy, rethinking subaltern urbanism requires more than just the inclusion of the narrative of the subaltern in the formation of theory. Indeed, it implies a paradigm shift in which the narratives of people are themselves taken as the production of knowledge. Rethinking subaltern urbanism is then both the reference and the vanishing point that establishes the slum and the periphery as theory.

With the title *Informalize!*, this publication recognizes in informal practices of subaltern urbanism a counter strategy against dominant modes of production, referencing research that responds to the global failure of the free market economy and the loss of governmental control. It attempts to read emerging urban structures as indicators of the processes of change that underlie urban growth and development. It traces the contours of an urban revolution that is taking place in the way we understand, produce, and sustain our everyday livelihoods. And, ultimately, it tries to grasp the prevailing determinants of urban form as a paradigmatic shift toward new ways of assembling and applying knowledge on the making of the city.

New housing settlements planned according to the Ecochard Grid materialize from the foundations of its dwellings. Carrières Centrales, 1952.

Accommodating the Afropolis: Michel Ecochard's Alternative Approach to the Modern City

By Tom Avermaete

Western urban forms, realities, and conditions still largely affect our understanding of how architects and urban designers can respond to urbanization and modernity. In particular, the European city, with its steady and controlled growth, has long served as the background against which new urban concepts and approaches are developed and evaluated. Meanwhile, global metropolitan regions grow relentlessly according to their own rationales; in African cities, for example, not only does the pace of urbanization differ significantly, but also its driving logic and processes. Nevertheless, architects and urban designers continue to use worn-out Western urban design tools and concepts in developing cities, turning a blind eye to the realities on the ground.

This text calls attention to another attitude towards modernity and urbanization that developed parallel to our Western approaches. Often out of sheer necessity, a group of urban planners and architects focused on different aspects of urbanization and subsequently developed alternative ways of analyzing and conceiving of urban development. These new attitudes neither idealize a final image of the modern city nor the complete control of the daily lives of its inhabitants. Rather, they engage with local actors and so-called informal developments to question the possible role of architects and urban designers.

A quintessential example of this alternative attitude can be found in the work of Michel Ecochard, whose biography reads as a fascinating tale of unique events, people, and places.[1] Educated as an archaeologist, architect, and urban planner in France, Ecochard practiced as an urban planner in Morocco, Senegal, Pakistan, and Syria, and collaborated with many key designers of his time, such as Le Corbusier, Constantine Doxiadis, Maxwell Fry, and Jane Drew. Ecochard also played a crucial role in the formulation of habitat policies for the United Nations.

Though at first glance his professional trajectory appears quite exceptional, I will argue that the figure of Ecochard is representative of a new type of urban planner that became active on the African continent in the period between 1950 and 1970. This new figure no longer plays the role of a local designer addressing familiar

---

1 An introduction to the work of Michel Ecochard can be found in articles by Eric Verdeil, among others: Eric Verdeil, "Michel Ecochard in Lebanon and Syria (1956-1968): The Spread of Modernism, the Building of the Independent States and the Rise of Local Professionals of Planning," *Science de l'Homme et de la Societe*, October 16, 2009, accessed on January 11, 2012, http://halshs.archives-ouvertes.fr/halshs-00424544/en/; and Eric Verdeil, "Une Ville et Ses Urbanistes: Beyrouth en Reconstruction," *Strates* 11 (2004), accessed on January 11, 2012, http://strates.revues.org/452. More information on the life of Ecochard can be found in the following sources: Joos Van Den Dool, "Le Rôle Professionnel de Michel Ecochard en Architecture, Archéologie et en Urbanisme Français à l'Étranger," PhD dissertation, University of Ghent, 2004; César Vabre, *Michel Ecochard: L'Influence du Climat dans la Démarche du Projet Architectural* (Paris: École d'Architecture de Paris-Belleville, 2007); Marion Leclercq and Marie-Jeanne Dumont, *L'Autre: Michel Ecochard, 1905-1985* (Paris: École d'Architecture de Paris-Belleville, 2007); Nathalie de Mazieres, "Homage," *Environmental Design: Journal of the Islamic Environmental Design Research Centre 1* (1985): 22-25.

cultural, social, and political forces. Rather, he specializes in international development and operates in a variety of geographical and cultural contexts, relentlessly engaging with new actors and interests. One of the most important characteristics of this new personality is that, by necessity, he or she uses a set of specific concepts, methods, and instruments that allow him or her to perform in a variety of contexts. This encompasses not only research methodologies, but also planning methods that engage local decision makers, architects, and construction workers, as well as versatile architectural typologies that can be built on a variety of terrains. Michel Ecochard's trajectory illustrates that this type of urban expert has done more than just develop a glocal toolbox of attitudes and approaches; more importantly, he has redefined the meaning of existing concepts and instruments in light of transnational development and, ultimately, he has challenged our Western attitudes toward modernity and urbanization.

A New Toolbox for Planning

Though Ecochard had been active in international development since the beginning of the thirties, the main breakthrough in his approach to planning came in the forties and fifties, within the context of the French Protectorate of Morocco. Since its establishment in 1912, the development of the Protectorate was spearheaded by the creation of ten *villes nouvelles*. In fact, these new towns, such as Casablanca, Rabat, Fes, and Marrakech, were key to Resident General Hubert Lyautey's valorisation strategy for the Moroccan territory.[2] The relationship of the city to the larger colonial political project continued to exist until the middle of the forties, when Eirik Labonne, the then Resident General, invited Ecochard to develop a firm urban policy for Morocco funded by the

2 Other important new towns include Meknes, Ouezanne, Port Lyautey (now Kenatra), Sefrou, Settat, and Taza.

1.1 billion dollars made available under the Marshall Plan.[3]

The general perception of Casablanca as a "potential center of nationalist fervor" galvanized General Labonne's support for Ecochard, naming him the director of the Service de l'Urbanisme and endowing him with "virtually dictatorial powers and ... a generous budget."[4,5] With an acclaimed team of French architects and planners at his disposal, Ecochard was instructed to study the urban structure of Morocco and the problems of informal housing—the so-called *bidonvilles*—in "the heartland of the colonial enterprise" that is Casablanca.[6] Between 1952 and 1960, the population of Casablanca had grown by 41 percent. Industrialization, coupled with the refusal of the Protectorate government to improve rural living conditions, encouraged people to move from the countryside to the city, which in turn fuelled urban growth.[7] By 1952, rural immigrants constituted three quarters of the city's population, causing a range of urban problems, such as overcrowding and poor sanitation.[8]

Because coastal Morrocan cities were expanding at a much faster rate than its inland towns, the French named a Delegate for Urban Affairs in seven cities and endowed these municipal officials with "broad powers in all matters related to security."[9] Planners and architects were

3 Former French colonies in North Africa were eligible for funds under the Marshall Plan. For a discussion on the topic, see Albert Waterston, *Planning in Morocco: Organization and Implementation* (Baltimore: Johns Hopkins Press, 1962), 7.
4 Planning and Development Collaborative International, "Upgrading of Marginal Neighborhoods in Morocco," (Rabat: Office of Housing and Urban Programs, Agency for International Development, USAID, 1983), 5.
5 Janet L. Abu-Lughod, *Rabat: Urban Apartheid in Morocco* (Princeton: Princeton University Press, 1980), 225.
6 *Ibid.*
7 The government's rejection of rural development was driven by their fear of decentralizing of power: "The hodgepodge of administration which allowed the French to have firm control previously, however, was difficult to translate into a new system [administrative apparatus], especially since the formation of regional and local representations implied more power and authority for Moroccans." Elaine C. Hagopian, "Conceptual Stability, the Monarchy, and Modernization in Morocco," *The Journal of Developing Areas 1* (1967): 205.
8 Hasan Awad, "Morocco's Expanding Towns," *The Geographical Journal* 130 (1967): 51.

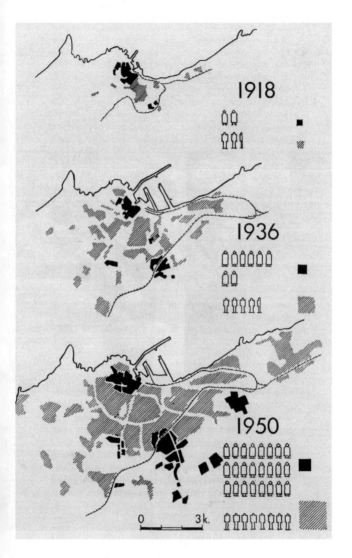

Fig.1: Diagram of population growth in Casablanca differentiating between
Muslim and non-Muslim inhabitants.

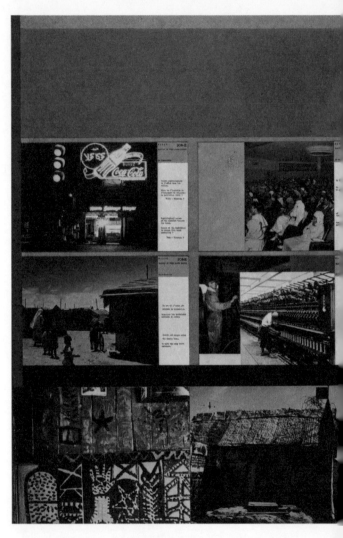

Fig.2: A survey of the *bidonvilles* conducted by the Service de l'Urbanisme and Michel Ecochard. Detail of GAMMA's Habitat du Plus Grand Nombre study, presented at the 9th congress of CIAM, Aix-en-Provence, France, 1953.

LE BIDONVILLE N'EST QU'UNE EXPRESSION......

LE PROBLEME HABITAT
EST PLUS VASTE

___ RESORPTION DES BIDONVILLES

___ DECONGESTION DES MEDINAS

___ SOLUTION A L'ACCROISSEMENT
DEMOGRAPHIQUE CONSTANT

called upon to devise design solutions to urban policing. In *Urbanization in Morocco*, Katherine Marshall Johnson, an urban scholar and historian, argues that "many were excellent men, yet the central concern of this system, quite explicitly, was security and the control of the population."[10]

The Survey: Mapping the Terrain and Establishing a Common Language

It is against the background of these political attempts to control the Moroccan territory and its inhabitants that Ecochard first started to develop his main urban planning tool: the survey or *enquête*.[11] The survey represented a way to understand the logic and interests of unfamiliar situations and to ultimately establish a solid base on which planning decisions could be made. In the words of Ecochard, the survey aimed "to analyze the problem within a wider framework, to get detailed knowledge about the industrial and social questions."[12] The large amount of surveys conducted by the Service de l'Urbanisme makes its central role in Ecochard's planning practice clear. Ecochard repeatedly referenced his survey in articles, books, and lectures, including *Casablanca: Roman d'une Ville*, published in 1955, and his presentation to the 9th Congres Internationale d'Architecture Moderne (CIAM) in Aix-en-Provence, 1953.[13] Together with the architects of the Atelier des Bâtisseurs, or ATBAT-Afrique, Ecochard presented a detailed investigation of Moroccan cities and their underlying rationales to CIAM's audience.

Ecochard's surveys were designed to analyze local

9 Katherine Marshall Johnson, *Urbanization in Morocco* (New York: Ford Foundation, 1972), 39.
10 *Ibid.* 40.
11 For a short introduction to the principles of the survey, see Michel Ecochard, "Les quartiers Industriels des Villes du Maroc," *Urbanisme* 11-12 (1951): 28.
12 *Ibid.*
13 Michel Ecochard, *Casablanca: Roman d'une Ville* (Paris: Editions de Paris, 1955).

situations on two scales: as a close reading of the physical characteristics of the terrain and as a critical analysis of local conditions within their broader political, financial, and social contexts. As such, and typical of Ecochard, the survey applies a wide variety of methods to evaluate urban conditions. At first, an urban phenomenon is analyzed quantitatively, evaluating the distribution of shantytowns, their degrees of urbanization, population densities, demographic trends, logics of internal migration, as well as the individual size and use of a shack in the bidonville. Collected data is then paired with diagrams, often developed by Ecochard himself. For Ecochard, the diagram is not only able to visualize logics and rationales in comparative ways. It can also articulate and clearly communicate the wider issues at stake to a larger audience. In fact, the strength of this first survey method is its ability to simultaneously inventory the local situation and communicate with local politicians, planners, and architects.

The second survey method, which consists of a fine and precise description of the actual terrain, is more qualitative by nature because it addresses ephemeral issues, such as collective and individual symbolism in the built environment and expressions of anti-colonial sentiment. To this end, Ecochard relies on the techniques of both photography and text. Photographic field research and documentation are in fact integral to Ecochard's approach to surveying and figured prominently in his presentation at the 9th CIAM congress. A large number of photographs taken from the ground—offering a view of the urban environment and its everyday appropriation—were shown and complemented with aerial photographs. These aerial photographs play a fundamental role in detecting the patterns and contours of urbanization, often the *terra incognita* within the context of colonial modernization.[14] In addition to photographs, texts are articulated in close affinity to the imagery produced.

14 In this domain, Ecochard's approach strongly reflects contemporary international studies, like those of Erwin Anton Gutkind. See Erwin Anton Gutkind, *Our World from the Air: An International Survey of Man and His Enviornment* (London: Chatto & Windus, 1952).

Short and concise statements not only provide commentary, but more importantly, a way to locate the photographs and their findings within their cultural, social, and political context:

> It is sufficient to interpret these documents carefully and confront the statistic data with plans and photographs of different dates. In that way, we ... can get a rather exact idea of the development ... it even offers us an order of magnitude for future planning.[15]

The final method combines both quantitative and qualitative analysis to provide a semi-rational frame of reference for the international expert and his team and a theoretical basis upon which his planning strategies, models, and projects can be based—all without being developed exclusively for the planner. Above all, the survey is meant to function as a mediator between the planner and local experts and decision makers. Indeed, through drawings, photography, and text, the survey defines the contours of an urban problem and articulates a shared planning issue that is to be tackled by the international expert in close collaboration with local actors. In addition, and perhaps most importantly, the survey establishes a joint conceptual basis—a lingua franca—that allows different actors to come together to discuss urban problems in a common language: "The results of this survey will be used for improving the efforts of engineers, architects, constructors ... in the domain of housing."[16]

Statements by Ecochard demonstrate that different political and technical professionals active in Morocco used

15 Ecochard, "Les Quartiers Industriels," 28.
16 Michel Ecochard, unpublished explanatory note to GAMMA Grid (1953), 2. The GAMMA Grid was presented by the Groupe d'Architectes Modernes Marocains, an association of architects working in Morocco that was active within the context of the Congrès International d'Architecture Moderne (CIAM) and included Georges Candilis and Michel Ecochard. At the occasion of the 9th CIAM in Aix-en-Provence, France, in 1953, this group delivered an impressive presentation that was titled GAMMA Grid of "Habitat for the Greatest Number."

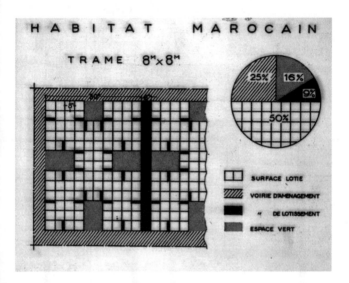

Fig.3: Principles of the 8 x 8 grid and its relation to public spaces
and different hierarchies of streets.

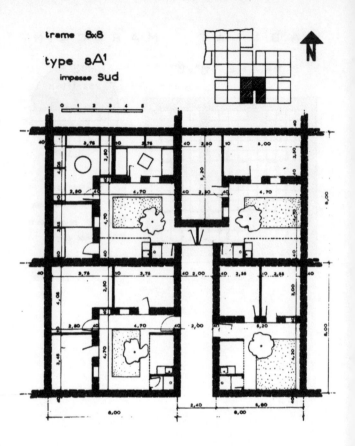

Fig.4: Different dwelling typologies accommodated by the 8 x 8 grid. Rooms
with a maximum width of three meters are configured around an open-air patio.

Fig.5: Model of the housing typologies in the 8 x 8 grid.
A 2.8 meter perimeter wall initially determines the plot size of each unit.

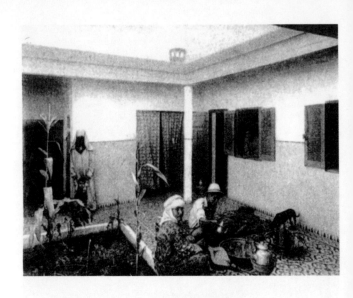

Fig.6: View of the patio that functions as a circulation space and a hallway, as well as an important outdoor living room, 1952.

the survey during the fifties to delineate and rephrase the problem of the bidonville.[17] While contemporary publications labeled the bidonville as a grave problem, with his survey, Ecochard managed to establish a more nuanced perspective and language: The bidonville was simultaneously defined by its problematic dwelling conditions and interesting forms of acculturation from rural dwelling patterns to urban life.

As the first indispensable exploration of what is often a complete *terrain vague* for the outsider expert, the role of the survey echoes the particular position of the international planning and development expert of the time. By describing the local situation, mapping the specificities of the terrain, and uncovering its underlying rationales, the survey established the basis and language necessary for the international planner to act and engage with his various interlocutors. This combination of a primal exploration of the site and the articulation of a new vocabulary transformed the survey into an instrument that allowed for new ways of seeing and understanding everyday situations. In fact, detached from the pressure of local power and politics, a fresh perspective on urban situations was and continues to be expected of the international planning expert.

The Hierarchised Grid: Design for Acculturation

Alongside the survey, the other most important instrument that Michel Ecochard developed as an international planning expert was the 8 × 8 meter grid, which formed the basic structure of a majority of his planning projects and was nicknamed *la Trame Ecochard* in Morocco.[18] The dimensions

---

17 A telling reference is a letter authored by Roger Maneville, head of the Delegation des Affaires Urbaines a Casablanca, to Ecochard, in which he writes that Ecochard's survey delineated the problems of the bidonville and offered a starting point for future action. Roger Maneville, head of Delegation des Affaires Urbaines a Casablanca, to Michel Ecochard, February 26, 1951, Archives Rabat, Rabat, Morocco.

Detail d'une trame d'habitations marocaines.

Fig.7: Aerial view of a vicinal unit with a variety of public spaces, such as boulevards (pictured at the bottom), streets, squares or *placettes*, and alleys.

of the 8 × 8 meter grid are not an obvious choice; however, in contrast to other contemporary planning methods that focused exclusively on parcelling and infrastructure, like the sites-and-services approach, it is clear that the grid was born out of an architectural approach to the city. In fact, each field in the grid corresponds to the figure of a low-rise patio dwelling with a total surface area of 64 square meters. Each dwelling is defined by a 2.8 meter perimeter wall, along which two or three rooms are located. Each of these rooms has a maximum width of three meters, which allows for simple construction with a variety of materials and methods. An open-air patio of at least five by five meters occupies the remainder of the unit and functions as both a circulation and access zone for the different rooms, as well as an important outdoor living room.

In drawings and collages, Ecochard illustrates the versatility of the grid, which not only combines different housing units, but also lays the foundation for basic infrastructure, like sewers, water wells, and roads. In other words, the grid creates what Ecochard refers to as the "ground storey frame," a framework that rationally and economically assembles and structures dwellings and infrastructure.[19] In addition, the 8 × 8 grid also streamlines the construction process. Photographs depicting the construction of several Moroccan neighborhoods planned according to the Ecochard Grid illustrate how the grid materializes from the foundations of each dwelling unit. The grid is traced on the site and subsequently built as a pattern of simple concrete foundations. With the basic foundations in place, the building and rebuilding of the neighborhood can take

18 A first description of this grid can be found in Jean Louis Cohen and Monique Eleb, *Casablanca: Mythes et Figures d'une Aventure Urbaine* (Paris: Hazan, 1998), translated and published in an English version: Jean Louis Cohen and Monique Eleb, *Casablanca: Colonial Myths and Architectural Ventures* (New York: Monacelli Press, 2003), as well as in Tom Avermaete, *Another Modern: The Post-War Architecture and Urbanism of Candilis-Josic-Woods* (Rotterdam: Nai Publishers, 2005).
19 See Groupe d'Architectes Modernes Marocains, "Habitat for the Greatest Number Grid," lecture presented at the 9th International Congress for Modern Architecture, Aix en Provence, 1953, panel 503-III.

Fig.8: A *placette* measuring twenty-four by sixteen meters, planted with trees
and designed for a collective life with one's immediate neighbors,
Carrières Centrales neighborhood, 1952.

Fig. 9: View of a street, Carrières Centrales neighborhood, 1952.

place. As such, the 8 × 8 grid provides the hardware for new urban development that conforms to standards of hygiene, economy, and transport; versatile, a series of different elements can be grafted to this basic hardware and grid.

Layering the Grid

What's most remarkable about the Ecochard Grid is that it is superimposed on several conceptual layers that are not global, but rather specific to the situation. An important conceptual layer that Ecochard projected on the basic grid was his notion on habitat and, more specifically, the neighborhood. Drawing on theories from the English-speaking world, such as Clarence Perry's neighborhood unit and Clarence Stein's neighborhood center, Ecochard developed his own version of the neighborhood.[20] In a circular scheme that strongly resembles those of his Anglo-Saxon predecessors, he depicts a neighborhood composed of five individual neighborhood units. Ecochard structures the neighborhood in a hierarchical composition. At the lowest level, a vicinal unit accommodates 1,800 inhabitants and everyday collective services, such as a mill, an oven, a playground for children, and shops.[21] Five of these vicinal or neighborhood units are arranged in a larger neighborhood of 9,000 people that is serviced by public facilities for commerce, markets and *fondouks*; worship, mosques and Koranic schools; administration and social services, police and health centers; recreation, hammams and theaters; and education, schools and kindergartens.

The neighborhood's hierarchy is physically articulated by the public spaces built into the Ecochard Grid. On the scale of the neighborhood unit, a network of alleys connect

20 Clarence Stein (1882-1975) and Clarence Perry (1872-1944) were American urban planners who contributed greatly to architectural theories on garden cities and neighborhood units. For an introduction to their work, see Peter Hall, *Urban and Regional Planning* (London: Routledge, 2002).
21 Ecochard based this number of 1,800 inhabitants on a study of market settlements and towns in North Africa.

Fig.10: The traditional *nouallas* were placed in the Ecochard Grid,
Fedala El Alia, 1952.

Fig.11: The transportation of a traditional hut from its rural location to the Ecochard Grid in the vicinity of the city.

little squares with a minimum dimension of 24 by 16 meters, commonly referred to as *placettes*. These little squares are planted with trees and designed to encourage a collective atmosphere among neighbors. Streets and avenues, as well as larger commercial squares with collective ovens, hammams, and main shops, are developed at the scale of the neighborhood. As a result, intricate networks of public spaces introduce a defined hierarchy of collectivity in Ecochard's Grid.

Engaging with Change and Evolution

Yet another conceptual layer woven into the 8 × 8 grid is that of change. The spatial evolution of neigborhoods was not just an interest of Ecochard's; on the contrary, it also figured prominently in contemporary projects by other international planning experts, including Koenigsberger, Doxiadis, Fry, and Drew. In fact, this collective interest in creating space for change can be read as an attempt to confront the tension between the transnational practice of the urban planner and the dynamism of local growth. After all, the success of the international expert depends largely on his ability to take into account variable and varying social, cultural, and financial conditions. With this perspective, Ecochard makes a clear distinction between the short-term temporality of architecture and the enduring legacy of urban planning: "Put the factors into order: Urbanism (permanent) in the first place, Construction (transitory) afterwards."[22] Construction, or architecture, is considered part of a process of continuous change; hence, Ecochard writes that "Moroccan Habitation, like any object of mass consumption, follows the cycle: conception, production, distribution, utilization, elimination. One must take this fact into consideration and one must be far-seeing."[23]

22 Groupe d'Architectes Modernes Marocains, "Habitat for the Greatest Number Grid," "The Problem."
23 *Ibid.*

In Ecochard's opinion, the built environment is subject to constant redefinition as a result of modernisation, changing economic conditions and aspirations, and fluctuating needs and forms associated to dwelling. Put plainly, evolutionary dwelling practices are coupled to evolving dwelling environments. Ecochard therefore describes the inhabitants of his projects as *evolués* who negotiate between a rural and an urban way of living. The built environment in which the evolué lives is viewed in an analogous and intermediate fashion: as a development that starts out as a rural formation and gradually becomes more urban in character. Ecochard illustrates his double perspective on the situation in a series of evolutionary sketches of an unnamed and abstract bidonville. The different drawings illustrate how the bidonville quickly upgrades from an improved shantytown that is structured and hygienic to a low-rise district and subsequently a high-rise neighborhood, which fully complies with an urban model of living.

Throughout this entire process of urban transformation, the grid belongs to the perennial realm of urbanism and provides a stable framework within which different physical and social transformations can occur. In his project for the town of Fedala El Alia, Ecochard shows how the grid can support both short-term and long-term planning by combining new infrastructure with more traditional approaches to housing. The same approach was applied to the rehousing of the Debagh Douar in Rabat. Both urban infrastructure and modern public amenities, such as baths, collective ovens, and so forth, were built in Rabat, while vernacular *nouallas* and huts were transported from their original rural locations to the maze of the city.

Ecochard also coined the grid for horizontal concentration and regarded it as the best possible approach to the rapidly growing and disperse peripheries of the Moroccan city. In order to maintain the qualities of horizontal concentration, Ecochard called for new legislation, *dahir* in Moroccan, to secure:

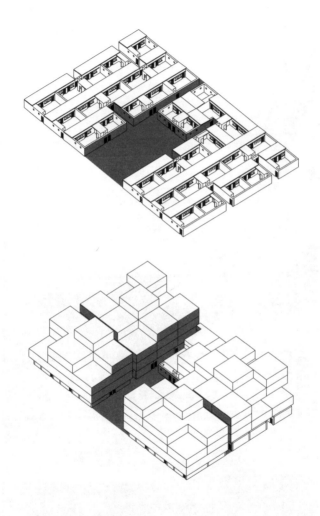

Fig.12: Transformation of a neighborhood unit and its public spaces.

Fig.13: Transformed neighborhood with several levels added to the original courtyard.

1. Green space or little squares, directly connected with the lodgings.
2. The minimum area of each bit of ground, that is to say 64 m^2 representing a vital minimum for each family with regard to housing.
3. The minimum area of the patio of 25 m^2, bringing in sunlight and air.
4. The limitation of the ground floor, according to a height of 2.80 m.
5. The minimum area of the units and openings.[24]

Together, Ecochard's grid, guidelines, and rules created a foundation both solid and flexible enough to accommodate changes in the needs, patterns, forms, and uses associated with dwelling. For Ecochard, this established an excellent base for future urban development.

The Perenniality of the Grid

In the past decades, the Ecochard Grid has left a decisive mark on the development of the metropolis of Casablanca. Indeed, despite the fact that Ecochard left Morocco as early as 1953 to take on other challenges and tasks, the grid system that he introduced remains one of the few stable factors in Moroccan urban planning. Even though its dimensions had been slightly adapted on occasion, the layered grid system was a mainstay of Moroccan urban planning up until the eighties; for thirty years, new urban and suburban residential neighborhoods all over Morocco were planned according to the Ecochard Grid.

The physical presence of the Ecochard Grid has proven to possess a remarkable perenniality and the importance that Ecochard paid to the different temporalities of architecture and urbanism has been prophetic. While Ecochard's urban grid is still omnipresent in Casablanca, the courtyard houses that were designed for it have almost entirely

24 GAMMA Grid, Panel 608-II.

disappeared. The grid has instead started to function as the basis for hypertrophied vertical urban growth, fuelled by both changing demographics and unbridled private speculation. Indeed, nowadays the single-level courtyard provides the foundation for three- to five-level terraced housing. All over the gridded neighborhoods of Casablanca, people have added concrete structures reminiscent of the Corbusian Domino System to their modest courtyard dwellings, thereby drastically intensifying and extending their houses vertically. A variety of infills within this common structure not only determine the interior organization of the house, but also its façade. This has resulted in a very diverse and vivid urban fabric, which is subject to incessant building and rebuilding, continuous change and adaptation.

Within this hypertrophied condition of change and densification, Ecochard's urban system has surprisingly maintained a certain quality of public space. Even though the streets and alleys that were originally proportioned to a single-level house now border buildings consisting of four storeys or more, as variants of the system of the medina, they still stand as a qualitative system of urban space. Designed to respond to the "unhygienic" conditions of the bidonville and the medina, after several decades of unfettered urban development, Ecochard's horizontal grid has succumbed to a condition very similar to that of its counter model. With its high, narrow streets and open squares surrounded by collective functions, the overgrown grid seems to comply with contemporary ways of dwelling in Casablanca: Its capacity to simultaneously accommodate private interest—densely developed residential blocks—alongside public interest—mass-circulation and public spaces—makes it a successful urban system.

The same can be said of the vertical extensions of the grid. Here, the initial aim of bringing light and fresh air into every room of the house has also been completely discarded by today's typology of terraced housing. Nevertheless, the figure of the vertically extendable terraced house seems to live up to contemporary aspirations and realities.

Indeed, many of the dwellings have been vertically enlarged to accommodate changing family compositions, needs, and values. For example, it is not uncommon that with the coming of age of each family member, a floor is added to the original house. Moreover, the renting of these additional floors has also secured a second source of income for many extended families.

Exporting the Grid

The approach to urban design developed in Casablanca is as much a reflection of Ecochard's career as a transnational development and planning expert as it is a reflection of Morocco's own urban development. After his resignation as the Director of the Service de l'Urbanisme in Casablanca, Ecochard would go on to illustrate that his approach to urban design can be applied in radically different geographical and political contexts.

The first occasion on which Ecochard reapplied his urban design approach dates to 1953, when he took a position as a consultant to the United Nations to design together with Constantine Doxiadis refugee housing near Karachi, the first federal capital of the newly established government of Pakistan. This project was funded by the Pakistani government and a host of international development agencies concerned with promoting stable allied governments in this critical region of the Cold War, including the UN, the Ford Foundation, and the International Cooperation Agency.[25] In this context, the refugee was a source of anxiety and a potential agent of revolution because of his undetermined status in the national context. And yet, even as an imminent threat, the refugee also presented a unique opportunity to suspend all political debate and pave a new path of social change and development exempt of political theater.

25 A description of this project can be found in Muhammad Iljal Muzaffar, *The Periphery Within: Modern Architecture and the Making of the Third World*, PhD, Massachusetts Institute of Technology, 2007.

In his presentation to the UN and the Pakistani government, Ecochard cited his Moroccan projects and especially the development of the 8 × 8 grid as major credentials. For Ecochard, the problems of refugee housing in Karachi bore strong similarities to the issues of rural-urban migration that he had faced in Casablanca. Here, as in Morocco, an encompassing survey of the city of Karachi was taken as a starting point for the project. In the survey, Ecochard framed the refugee problem within the context of the growing density and increased mobility caused by the modernization of Pakistan. As a result, the design for the refugee settlement did more than just shelter. It also established an evolving framework that could accommodate shifts in density and that complied with different degrees of modernization and standards of living. Much as for the bidonvilles in Casablanca, Ecochard saw in the refugee and his habitat a figure that epitomized the national transition between tradition and modernity, painting his own approach and its international support as custodians of the gradual, coordinated growth and transformation of a nation.

A second occasion on which Ecochard was able to deploy his specific method was when he was invited to design the master plan for Dakar, Senegal, in 1963, only three years after the former colony gained its independence from France.[26] In Dakar, too, Ecochard identified rural-urban migration as the central framework through which new urban development had to be considered. Ecochard's project proposed the renovation of the old city and its existing neighborhoods—Reubeus, Médina, Grand Dakar, and Pikine—as well as the design of new districts that could accommodate a continuous stream of immigrants.

In Senegal, Ecochard remained faithful to earlier urban plans for the capital. The starting point was again a thorough survey that mapped the different rationales and plans for urban development in Dakar. On the basis of results ob-

26 Michel Ecochard, "L'Urbanisme dans les Pays en Voie de Development et la Cooperation Vue en Sens le Plus Large," *L'Architecture d'Aujourd'hui* 132 (1967): 104.

tained during a period of three years, Ecochard developed a regular grid that functioned as a foundation for large parts of the city. In Dakar, the grid was used to integrate new urban neighborhoods with earlier urban interventions that were based on Haussmannian ideals. Just as in Morocco, the grid functioned as a framework that absorbed the evolving exigencies of the terrain and situation. The Dakar project was designed to accommodate a population growth of up to 1.2 million inhabitants by 1980. And, once again, this enormous urban growth was structured through neighborhoods characterized by a particular hierarchy of public spaces.

In the Protectorate of Morocco, the grid had provided the means to improve the poor housing conditions experienced by new urban immigrants; in Senegal, however, it also became the foundation of a modernization project that encompassed the development of industry and tourism, as well as educational facilities, an Olympic stadium, and a mosque. The Ecochard Grid bound these elements of the economy and society, the profane and religious, together in the figure of a modern and encompassing African city: the Afropolis for the greatest number.

Transnational Experts and Alternative Approaches

Although unique, Ecochard's trajectory on the African continent reflects and illuminates the emergence of a new protagonist of post-war architecture: the transnational development and planning expert. Indeed, during the fities and the sixties, a newfangled expert appeared on the African continent, providing plans for developing metropolises and regions and always inextricably linked to the logic of decolonialization and the cold war politics of the time. Figures like Charles Abrams, Otto Koenigsberger, Constantine Doxiadis, Max Fry, and Jane Drew embodied this new character. They were experts without a local base; instead, their practices grew transnationally as they moved from one region to another, often attempting to balance local realities on the ground with broader international interests.

Most importantly, the work of these experts shaped a different attitude towards modernity and urbanization. In the work of Ecochard and his fellow transnational colleagues, another type of Modernism becomes manifest. Unlike mainstream Western urban planning, this new approach is neither focused on the architect's vision nor obsessed with idealized living environments and building methods; its goal is to engage a diverse set of actors and to accommodate a variety of evolving ways of dwelling and building. Hence, one of the most important characteristics of this new attitude is its use of traditional idioms of architectural form, as well as the language of finance, sociology, and community development. As a matter of fact, the strength of the development and planning expert of the time was measured by his ability to incorporate the individual idioms of a variety of urban actors in his planning instruments. As such, the central role of the survey in Ecochard's practice provides an important case in point. Not only did it attempt to map the local terrain; above all, it established a language that was able to articulate a rich and varied geographic, economic, social, and spatial context through a common vocabulary. It is this vocabulary that allowed Ecochard's planning projects to resonate throughout a vast territory and among its many urban actors.

Responding to the edge condition of rapidly growing African cities, the transnational planner needed instruments, concepts, and models that could easily adapt to shifting terrains and changing demographics. In retrospect, however, this new practice offered a point of departure to rethink the modern in architecture as no longer defined trough static, detailed, and finalized images of the built environment, but as an ongoing development of urban processes of transformation, appropriation, and acculturation. Ultimately, with his focus on the spatial practices of dwelling and building, Ecochard tried to develop a modern design strategy capable of grasping the urban edge—its dynamic character and ambiguity. Five decades later, and under drastically different conditions, Ecochard's grid still provides the foundations for everyday life in Casablanca. Having designed a frame within which a proper African urbanity can develop, Ecochard and his transnational practice will forever remain part of the effort to accommodate the Afropolis.

An earlier version of this essay was first published under the title "Framing the Afropolis: Michel Ecochard and the African City for the Greatest Number" in *OASE* 82 (2010): 77-101.

Bibliography:

Abu-Lughod, Janet L. *Rabat: Urban Apartheid in Morocco*. Princeton: Princeton University Press, 1980.

Avermaete, Tom. *Another Modern: The Post-War Architecture and Urbanism of Candilis-Josic-Woods*. Rotterdam: Nai Publishers, 2005.

Awad, Hasan. "Morocco's Expanding Towns." *The Geographical Journal* 130 (1967): 49-64.

Cohen, Jean Louis and Monique Eleb. *Casablanca: Colonial Myths and Architectural Ventures*. New York: Monacelli Press, 2003.

——. *Casablanca: Mythes et Figures d'une Aventure Urbaine*. Paris: Hazan, 1998.

De Mazieres, Nathalie. "Homage." *Environmental Design: Journal of the Islamic Environmental Design Research Centre* 1 (1985): 22-25.

Ecochard, Michel. "L'Urbanisme dans les Pays en Voie de Development et la Cooperation Vue en Sens le Plus Large." *L'Architecture d'Aujourd'hui* 132 (1967): 19-21.

——. *Casablanca: Roman d'une Ville*. Paris: Editions de Paris, 1955.

——. Unpublished note to Groupe d'Architectes Modernes Marocains. 1953.

——. "Les Quartiers Industriels des Villes du Maroc." *Urbanisme* 11-12 (1951): 25-39.

Groupe d'Architectes Modernes Marocains. "Habitat for the Greatest Number Grid." Lecture, 9th International Congress for Modern Architecture, Aix en Provence. 1953.

Gutkind, Erwin Anton. *Our World from the Air: An International Survey of Man and His Enviornment*. London: Chatto & Windus, 1952.

Hagopian, Elaine C. "Conceptual Stability, the Monarchy, and Modernization in Morocco." *The Journal of Developing Areas* 1 (1967).

Hall, Peter. *Urban and Regional Planning*. London: Routledge, 2002.

Johnson, Katherine Marshall. *Urbanization in Morocco*. New York: Ford Foundation, 1972.

Leclercq, Marion and Marie-Jeanne Dumont. *L'Autre: Michel Ecochard, 1905-1985*. Paris: École d'Architecture de Paris-Belleville, 2007.

Maneville, Roger. Head of Delegation des Affaires Urbaines a Casablanca, to Michel Ecochard. February 26, 1951. Archives Rabat, Rabat, Morocco.

Muzaffar, M. Iljal. "The Periphery Within: Modern Architecture and the Making of the Third World." PhD, Massachusetts Institute of Technology, 2007.

Planning and Development Collaborative International. "Upgrading of Marginal Neighborhoods in Morocco." Rabat: Office of Housing and Urban Programs, Agency for International Development, USAID, 1983.

Vabre, César. *Michel Ecochard: L'Influence du Climat dans la Démarche du Projet Architectural*. Paris: École d'Architecture de Paris-Belleville, 2007.

Van Den Dool, Joos. "Le Rôle Professionnel de Michel Ecochard en Architecture, Archéologie et en Urbanisme Français à l'Étranger." PhD dissertation, University of Ghent, 2004.

Verdeil, Eric. "Une Ville et Ses Urbanistes: Beyrouth en Reconstruction." *Strates* 11 (2004). Accessed on January 11, 2012. http://strates.revues.org/452.

Verdeil, Eric. "Michel Ecochard in Lebanon and Syria (1956-1968): The Spread of Modernism, the Building of the Independent States and the Rise of Local Professionals of Planning." *Science de l'Homme et de la Societe*. October 16, 2009, accessed on January 11, 2012. http://halshs.archives-ouvertes.fr/halshs-00424544/en/.

Waterston, Albert. *Planning in Morocco: Organization and Implementation*. Baltimore: Johns Hopkins Press, 1962.

An informal street market in Paraisópolis,
one of São Paulo's largest favelas.

Informality
and Its Discontents

By
Fran Tonkiss

The World As Jerry-built

The idea of the informal reverses the colonial tendencies
of the urban imagination, travelling across the old geographies of urban power from global south to global north,
from margin to center. At a broad scale, this is because the
major plot line in the story of contemporary urbanization
is one of informality. In both the material making of cities
and the social organization of urban economies, most rapid
urban growth today is informal—either partly or wholly
beyond the reach of governments and outside the shadow
of the law. Even the state-led city-building of the Chinese
boom has relied on a large informal sector of unregistered
and unprotected migrant laborers. At more local scales,
the big picture of urban informality highlights how much of
urban life takes place off-the-books, without planning permits and in defiance of any regulation. In simple terms, this
is the way a very great number of people in the urbanized
world *do* cities.

Urban informality has most often been associated with
cities in the developing world, but questions of informality
do not only impact on the urban poor. The ongoing retreat
of the state has animated political debate and shaped
urban processes around informality (or less formality, even

anti-formality) in many high-income countries. While a language of informality may now translate between poor and rich world cities, it plays out rather differently in each context. What once was a matter of subsistence or survivalist urbanism is now seen as a key driver of urban growth in the developing world, whether we think about such growth in terms of economics, demographics, or the city's physical footprint. Much emerging economic trade is "unconventional," many incoming urban residents are undocumented, and a majority of new building activity is illegal. The relationship between informality and urban growth is inverted in advanced capitalist cities. While working or living in the cracks between the formal and informal has long been understood as what some migrants, many chancers, and a few hippies do, informality has taken on a new salience with the crisis in economic growth, as governments retrench, jobs dry up, and development sites lay empty.

In economic settings, informal practices are often invisible, connoting under-the-counter trade, unaccounted income, and clandestine workplaces. In contrast, informal processes shape patterns of urban settlement and urban form in more observable ways. As urban informality gets built out, it becomes visible in the physical order of the city, regardless of whether informal settlements are represented on official maps. In many cases, the spatial logic of informality is that of densification, especially the infill of tight spaces in consolidated parts of the city. A counter-logic of informality is that of sprawl, the spread of peripheral developments on the urban outskirts, whether at points of arrival or of exclusion at the city limits. In this sense, the urban geography of marginality can be found as much at the city's center as on its edge. Writing about Lagos, Matthew Gandy goes beyond the language of sprawl to talk about an "amorphous urbanism": The mutable form of a "city that is simultaneously growing, dividing, polarizing and decaying," and in which lines of formality and informality are threaded through the complicated fabric of the city.[1]

1 Matthew Gandy, "Learning from Lagos," *New Left Review* 33 (2005): 52.

If accelerated urbanization has remade "the planet as building site," as David Harvey suggests, then it is one that is largely undocumented, casualized, and makeshift.[2] Put plainly, the urban world is jerry-built. Informality today is not simply one "idiom of urbanization," but its first language.[3] Nor is this effect solely due to the urbanization of and by the poor. Informality, in cities like Karachi, Istanbul, and Cairo, "has become a primary avenue for home ownership for the lower-middle and middle classes," as well as a significant opportunity for the landlord classes everywhere.[4]

The jerry-built city is necessarily an inventive one. Outsider urbanism, or urbanization from below, is increasingly celebrated for its tactical and resourceful colonization of space, as well as its clever economies and unruly sociability. Informal spaces have become test sites for "new ideas unfettered by law or tradition," as the environmentalist Stewart Brand argues: "Alleyways in squatter cities, for example, are a dense interplay of retail and services—one-chair barbershops and three-seat bars interspersed with the clothes racks and fruit tables."[5] Such a make-do attitude offers a model for the creative reuse of dead spaces in the formal city. Brand cites Jaime Lerner, the former Mayor of Curitiba, Brazil, and all-around poster boy for urban innovation: "Allow the informal sector to take over downtown areas after 6 P.M. ... That will inject life into the city."[6]

Drawing lessons from informality—or "learning from Tijuana," as Teddy Cruz puts it—is partly about taking seriously the intensities of activity and interaction that Cruz recommends as a finer measure of urban density than

2 David Harvey, "The Right to the City," *New Left Review* 53 (2008): 37.
3 Ananya Roy, "Strangely Familiar: Planning and the Worlds of Insurgence and Informality," *Planning Theory* 8.1 (2009): 9.
4 Nezar AlSayyad, "Urban Informality As a 'New' Way of Life," in *Urban Informality: Transnational Perspectives from the Middle East, Latin America, and South Asia*, edited by Ananya Roy and Nezar AlSayyad (Lanham, MD.: Lexington Books, 2004), 24.
5 Stewart Brand, "How Slums Can Save the Planet," *Prospect* (February 2010): 40.
6 *Ibid.*

any standard population count.[7] Informality is productive, opening up alternatives in the over-programmed and
over-capitalized cities of the rich world by injecting life
into downtowns or offering off-beat solutions to living in
saturated property markets and depressed labor markets.
Spaces of disuse and dereliction, as well as opportunities
for appropriation, can be found in virtually every city. A
growing recognition of the informal, temporary, and improvised as the backdrop for urban innovation has provided
a platform for amateur and unsolicited designers to make
space on the hop, the sly, or the cheap: a kind of architecture without architects *with* architects, if you will. But
there is a great difference between the DIY urbanism of a
resting creative class in the cities of the rich world and the
subsistence strategies of get-by urbanism in the cities of
the poor. New myths of marginality have emerged around
the aesthetics of the informal, the romance of the slum, and
the allure of the urban edge.[8]

Informality from Above

Spaces of informality may be linked with practices of
insurgency, resistance, and the "quiet encroachment" of
the poor and ignored upon the city.[9] But the recourse to
informality is also a routine tactic of the powerful. As we
know, the rich are not much given to paying taxes; the off-
balance sheet activities of the advanced financial sector

7 Teddy Cruz, "Trans-border Flows: An Urbanism Beyond the Property Line,"
in *Urban Transformation*, edited by Ilka Ruby and Andreas Ruby (Berlin: Ruby
Press, 2008).
8 See Ananya Roy, "Transnational Trespassing: The Geopolitics of Urban
Informality," in *Urban Informality: Transnational Perspectives from the Middle
East, Latin America, and South Asia*, edited by Ananya Roy and Nezar AlSayyad
(Lanham, MD.: Lexington Books, 2004), 289-312; cf. Janice Perlman, *The Myth
of Marginality: Urban Poverty and Politics in Rio de Janeiro* (Berkeley, CA.:
University of California Press, 1976).
9 Asef Bayat, "From 'Dangerous Classes' to 'Quiet Rebels': Politics of the
Urban Subaltern in the Global South," *International Sociology* 15.3 (2000):
533-557.

have proved a match for even the murkiest underground economy. The other side of equity planning is a skewed form of planning for elites that passes under the guise of formal neutrality. In both advanced and emerging market economies, urban-planning-as-usual is too often a version of advocacy planning for the largest speculators and developers, nodded through by captive officials and eased on its way by sympathetic politicians or princes.

In a stark context of spatial injustice, Oren Yiftachel draws on the case of Israel and Palestine to define the "stratification" of informalities as the determination of which illegalities can be condoned and which cannot.[10] This is to differentiate the "informality of the powerful," the kind of extra-legality that allows for the arbitrary exercise of spatial control, from the illegality of the powerless.[11] In other words, your claims to space are unrecognized, undocumented, and illegitimate; *my* occupation of space is a reality on the ground. Similarly, in the context of Calcutta, Ananya Roy argues that the power to make and re-make space is not simply the preserve of formal zoning, but also evident in the casual "unmapping" of existing land uses and property and development rights.[12] The rule of law in cities is not only required to give ordinary, vulnerable, and marginal citizens a basis for making claims on formal institutions, but also to protect them against the prerogatives of informality from above.[13]

As an idiom of urbanization, the language of informality only crudely translates from Cairo's City of the Dead or Kibera in Nairobi to Christiania in Copenhagen; between the "informality" of Israeli settlement-building in the Oc-

10 Oren Yiftachel, "Theoretical Notes on 'Gray Cities': The Coming of Urban Apartheid?" *Planning Theory* 8.1 (2009): 88–100.
11 *Ibid.*
12 Ananya Roy, "The Gentleman's City: Urban Informality in the Calcutta of the New Communism," in *Urban Informality: Transnational Perspectives from the Middle East, Latin America, and South Asia*, edited by Ananya Roy and Nezar AlSayyad (Lanham, MD.: Lexington Books, 2004), 147-170.
13 See Gerald Frug, "A 'Rule of Law' for Cities," *Urban Age Mumbai Newspaper Essay*, 2007, accessed January 17, 2012. http://www.urban-age.net/0_downloads/archive/_mumbai/Newspaper-essays_Frug.pdf.

cupied Territories and that of Palestinian refugee camps in Jordan and Lebanon;[14] and from the "quiet encroachment of the ordinary" to more invasive and overbearing spatial claims by the privileged. In the remainder of this article, I want to consider in more detail informality's contradictions: the double-edge of a set of economic and spatial processes that might help us trace the contours of both contemporary urbanism and "the city yet to come."[15] Roy contends that "in the ever-shifting relationship between what is legal and illegal, legitimate and illegitimate, authorized and unauthorized, informality is a state of exception and ambiguity."[16] I aim to identify here some aspects of this ambiguity, the tensions that run through informality and its discontents.

The Contradictions of Informality
1. Organic settlement/Slum

From a sociological standpoint, informality is something of a non-concept. A lack of formality does not denote a lack of organization. Whether or not they are regulated by explicit or legal codes, socio-spatial practices and human settlements are always subject to rules. Indeed, tacit norms and social conventions can be far more effective in organizing behavior and ordering spaces than legal systems. The formal and the informal may or may not be categorical distinctions in law, but they are rarely clearly distinguished in social life. A similarly basic opposition in the study of urban morphology differentiates "organic" patterns of settlement from those that are planned. The former are understood as adaptive: responding to environmental conditions and limits, organized around habitual patterns of movement,

14 See Romola Sanyal, "Squatting in Camps: Building and Insurgency in Spaces of Refuge," *Urban Studies* 48.5 (2011): 877–890.
15 See Abdoumaliq Simone, *For the City Yet to Come: Changing African Life in Four Cities* (Durham, NC.: Duke University Press, 2004); and Robert Neuwirth, "Squatters and the Cities of Tomorrow," *City* 11.1 (2007): 71-80.
16 Roy, "Strangely Familiar," 8.

and reproducing social solidarities. One of the key critical arguments for informal modes of settlement has focused on these qualities and their capacity to support different uses, as well as a physical flexibility that allows for their extension and conversion. This argument is reflected in both John Turner's advocacy in the seventies for the "supportive shack" as better than the "oppressive house" in meeting the needs of Mexico City's urban poor and more recent opposition to the redevelopment and resettlement of Dharavi and other informal settlements in Mumbai.[17]

These are compelling arguments, which underline the ambiguity of porous housing environments that are accommodating and adaptable, but also physically permeable and legally vulnerable. The United Nation's definition of a slum is based on five simple forms of "shelter deprivation": lack of access to improved water; lack of access to sanitation; non-durable housing; insufficient living area; and insecurity of tenure. The measure brings together environmental, physical, and legal forms of insecurity, highlighting the complex character of informality as a material condition and a legal construct. Moreover, these forms of shelter deprivation are hardly confined to slum housing in poor cities. In terms of improvements in urban housing, the modern narrative of progress has stalled in cities like London, Paris, and New York as public housing is privatized or degraded, private property markets spiral out of reach for low-income households, and new generations of slum landlords prey on migrant populations. The UN's fifth criterion of shelter deprivation—insecurity of tenure—is the hardest to define, especially where legal systems of private property and communal or traditional rights overlap, property and possession stake out different claims to space, and the right to housing is understood outside the letter of legal title.

17 John Turner, *Housing by People: Towards Autonomy in Building Environments* (London: Marion Boyars, 1976).

2. Self-help/Abandonment

It has become conventional to argue that the informal economy is neither residual nor marginal, but rather the most dynamic sector of any rapidly growing economy. "If people mattered," Manuel Castells argues, "the informal economy would be treated as the real economy," given the numbers it supports, the range of goods and services it provides, and its functional relationship to the formal sector.[18] Nor is formality and informality a meaningful way of differentiating developed from developing economies: A large part of the material needs of people in advanced economies is met through informal and largely undocumented activities in caring and domestic labor, self-provisioning and mutual aid, doing favors and lending money, cadging, hustling, and so on.

The economics of self-help has a long history among poor urban populations and, in particular, groups that experience systematic forms of economic exclusion, notably women and minorities.[19] In this sense, the recourse to self-help by groups shut out from mainstream labor or credit markets, either by discrimination or disregard, can be read as a survivalist response to economic abandonment: This is the enterprise of exclusion. Indeed, the economics of self-help can reinforce and embed the very kind of exclusion and social abandonment that it seeks to overcome, as the self-employed get by without access to welfare rights, reliable credit, pension entitlements, labor protections, and trading licenses, even as they provide goods and services—as street vendors, petty producers, or domestic laborers—to the formal economy. Micro-credit offers a key instance in which self-help strategies from the developing world have translated into international models for

18 Manuel Castells, "Why the Mega-cities Focus?" *The Mega-Cities Project Publication* MCP-018 (1998).
19 See Alejandro Portes, Manuel Castells and Lauren A. Benton, eds., *The Informal Economy: Studies in Advanced and Less Developed Economies* (Baltimore, MD.: Johns Hopkins University Press, 1989); WWF, *Social Platform Through Social Innovations: A Coalition with Women in the Informal Sector* (Chennai: Working Women's Forum, 2000).

small-scale economic development. Systems of mutual and rotating credit are an important resource for those who lack access to formal financial institutions, but so is the loan shark. Hernando de Soto has convinced as many as he has antagonized with his analysis of "dead capital."[20] He argues that since housing and other physical assets in informal settlements are not based on formal property rights, their latent value cannot be realised and, therefore, used for investment or to provide collateral for a loan. Between self-help and abandonment, micro-credit institutions and groups, like the Self-Employed Women's Association (SEWA) and the Working Women's Forum (WWF)—both founded in India to establish basic rights and entitlements for women workers, with trade unions as their models—attempt to organize (indeed, to formalize) informal economic activities. These economic strategies work in the uncertain spaces between petty capitalism and mutualism, subsistence and enterprise, which make any clear distinction between the formal and informal hard to sustain.

3. Social capital/Racketeering

Economic strategies of self-help frequently rely on social networks to access resources, including credit, information, land, physical capital, protection, labor, or work opportunities. The informal mobilization of social capital allows people to find work, make space, borrow money, stay safe, and acquire goods in a way that would not be possible if individuals had to rely on such formal networks as credit unions, consumer and labor markets, formal private and public housing, and police and welfare systems. Like so much else in the field of informality, the use of social ties for economic purposes is hardly a tactical approach confined to the poor. Urban elites are probably most adept at capitalizing on their social networks outside of formal systems of employment and preferment, contracting and

20 Hernando de Soto, *The Mystery of Capital* (London: Black Swan, 2001).

financing. Reliance on informal networks becomes more widely relevant as increasing privatization in both low- and high-income economies sees the "public goods which provide formal security disappear, and for the great majority, informal provision of formerly public goods becomes a condition of survival."[21]

That social capital has a dark side has become a commonplace assertion. Forms of closure, exclusion and compulsion—the inequitable structuring of informal networks—tend to bear most heavily on the poorest, for whom informal strategies are not an alternative to formal markets, contracts, and institutions, but, in fact, the only market (Castells' "real economy" in money, work, and land). Social networks that are not regulated by law, like those that are, are subject to capture, duress, intimidation, and stand-over tactics. As Gandy argues, any serious account of an informal economy cannot "ignore its highly hierarchical, often coercive structures" or fail to "differentiate between the mini (or even major) entrepreneurs and traders on its summits and the mass of those barely surviving at its base."[22] The line between an informal network and a property or protection racket is a fine one, as property mafias and a variety of other informal "entrepreneurs and parasites" fill the spaces evacuated or never colonized by the formal market or the state.[23, 24] Here, people may have little recourse to protection under the law or from (and often against) the police.

4. Temporary use/Insecurity

Informality has a complex relation to impermanence. While informal settlements represent what Jon Unruh calls

21 Elmar Altvater, "Globalization and the Informalization of Urban Space," in *Informal City: Caracas Case*, edited by Alfredo Brillembourg, Kristin Feiress and Hubert Klumpner (Munich: Prestel Verlag, 2005), 53.
22 Gandy, "Learning from Lagos," 46-7.
23 See Jon D. Unruh, "Debates: Urbanization in the Developing World and the Acutely Tenure Insecure," *City* 11.1 (2007): 115-120.

"acutely insecure real estate," many slums, favelas, *chabolas*, and *gecekondular* are long-standing parts of their urban environments, predating and often outlasting legal housing developments.[25] Radical insecurity can coexist with relative permanence. Squatters' rights—where these can be claimed—require the test and testimony of time. "Temporary" structures can prove highly resilient.

One part of the idiom of informality that has translated more widely into current approaches to urbanism is the emphasis on temporary uses of space—urban improvisations that occupy and activate spaces of disuse or desertion. These tactics draw on the gestures of the informal and provisional, finding spatial opportunities for commerce, art, and dwelling in unlikely and unofficial sites.[26] This kind of urbanism recalls the spatial politics of squatting in cities like London, Amsterdam, Copenhagen, and Berlin, where long-established squats have been evicted and the practice itself is increasingly proscribed. In post-crisis London, "meanwhile uses" have been promoted by the Mayor to animate stalled development sites and inject life into leftover spaces; at the same time, the national government has moved to make squatting a criminal offence. As temporary uses of disused or undeveloped sites move from the realm of improvisation to that of policy, unauthorized informality in the form of Occupy protests or squatting of empty properties has been subject to clean-up and crackdown. There is a vast difference between pop-ups in the recessionary spaces of rich-world cities and teardowns in the informal settlements of the poor. But they share something in common beyond the language of informality: both disappear in the face of more valuable uses.

24 Simone, *For the City Yet to Come.*
25 Unruh, "Debates," 116.
26 See Philipp Oswalt, Klaus Overmayer, and Philipp Misselwitz, eds., *Urban Catalyst: Strategies for Temporary Use* (Barcelona: Actar, 2009).

5. "Looseness"/Disorder

If tactics of informality in the cities of the poor are a response to the absence of the state, in rich-world cities the idiom of informality is more often than not a challenge to the excessive regulation of space. In over-planned and over-programmed cities where public and private zones are clearly demarcated, lines of ownership and access highly secured, and different functions and behaviors tightly prescribed, the room for spatial maneuvering is limited. In response, recent approaches to urbanism have focused on the potential of "loose space" that is not wholly legible and which might provide spaces of contingency with the capacity to support the unexpected, provisional, and unplanned.[27] This approach draws on a strain of urban theory open to the "uses of disorder" in the city, highlighting the social value and urban freedoms afforded by unlikely encounters and unruly spaces.[28]

While conventional approaches to urban design may have overemphasized the legibility of space, disorder also has its downside. It may be an urban skill to read situations that are uncertain or volatile, but pleasurable disorder can be experienced simply as danger by those who, in terms of gender, age, race, or culture, fall on the wrong side of the informal codes that structure "loose" spaces. It is worth repeating that social space is always subject to some version of order, however provisional, precarious, or unspoken. In the absence of explicit and enforceable laws, tacit rules can serve to support different uses and accommodate different kinds of bodies in space, but they can also reinforce expressions of power and lines of exclusion that are no less punitive because they are "informal." In many spatial contexts, after all, there are no formal rules that state that men have a greater claim to space than women do, that young people can intimidate the old or the weak, or that the

27 See Karen Franck and Quentin Stevens, eds., *Loose Space: Possibility and Diversity in Urban Life* (London: Routledge, 2006).
28 See Richard Sennett, *The Uses of Disorder: Personal Identity and City Life* (New York: Knopf, 1970).

self-appointed representatives of racial or cultural majorities can harass or exclude minorities; and yet these are routine ways in which a tacit order of space is maintained by informal norms and unwritten codes.

6. Commonalty/Invasive publicness

Spaces of informality call into question the conventional distinctions between public and private that structure social environments. As an ideal and in practice, the politics of informality contests both the appropriation of space by private property and the spatial prerogatives of the state. It seeks to expand the range of land, things, and resources that can be commonable—whether through the collective occupation of space, shared access to goods, or the illicit de-privatization of water, electricity, and oil by tapping into formal networks. This is perhaps the most critical register in the idiom of urban informality: the claim that there are alternative and more basic ways of organizing space than through the division between public and private. The contradictions of informality are also particularly acute here, as spaces that are shared but not owned are vulnerable to a number of tragedies of the commons—theft, blight, conflict, over-consumption, and neglect.

The other side of commonalty is an invasive publicness that precludes even the most minimal amount of privacy. Some fifty years ago, Charles Abrams despaired that "in the age of the atom, the disposal of human feces remains one of the stubbornly persistent problems of urban man."[29] It's even worse for urban women. The enduring "politics of shit" is one of the most basic examples of the challenges associated with living outside the legal and physical infrastructure of public and private.[30] How is it possible for individuals and households, especially women and

29 Charles Abrams, *Man's Struggle for Shelter in an Urbanizing World* (Cambridge, MA.: MIT Press, 1964), 5.
30 See Arjun Appadurai, "Deep Democracy: Urban Governmentality and the Horizon of Politics," *Public Culture* 14.1 (2002): 21-47.

their dependents, to protect their privacy and property in conditions of radical commonalty? In severe conditions of overcrowding, with minimal to no sanitation, or in extreme shelter deprivation, the distinction between the public and private is collapsed into a stark commonalty lacking both the protections of the private and the dignities of the public.

Informality and Its Discontents

In the mid-nineties, Rem Koolhaas wrote that "the city's defiant persistence and apparent vigor, in spite of the collective failure of all the agencies that act on it or try to influence it—creatively, logistically, politically" had proved "'disconcerting and (for architects) humiliating."[31] This lament for modern urbanism overlooked the single most important form of agency in the city: the "ordinary" inhabitants who continuously make and re-make their cities, if rarely under circumstances of their own choosing. Persistent and vigorous like the city itself, these actors engage in the logistics and politics of urban life in ways that go beyond the plan, commission, and competition entry, and well beyond any easy distinction between the formal and informal.

As an idiom of urbanization, informality translates more or less into different contexts. In contrast to the survivalist strategies of the urban poor in cities of inequality, exclusion, and abandonment, the use of the language of the informal to describe creative interventions in spaces of urban privilege seems absurd, if not obscene. And, yet, the withdrawal of the state and the uneven advance of privatization produces spaces of desertion and potential in both developed and developing cities. The challenge goes beyond finding spaces for informality in highly regulated cities or securing the urbanism of informality in the cities of the poor. It raises the question of how different spaces of commonalty might work—"creatively, logistically,

31 Rem Koolhaas, "Whatever Happened to Urbanism?" in *S,M,L,XL*, edited by Rem Koolhaas and Bruce Mau (New York: The Monicelli Press, 1995).

politically"—in different sites. Those who seek to act on the city and influence it must address the shifting tensions between improvisation and insecurity, creativity and contingency, the provisional and the precarious—the complex spatialities of informality and its discontents.

Bibliography:

Abrams, Charles. *Man's Struggle for Shelter in an Urbanizing World*. Cambridge, MA.: MIT Press, 1964.

AlSayyad, Nezar. "Urban Informality As a 'New' Way of Life." In *Urban Informality: Transnational Perspectives from the Middle East, Latin America, and South Asia*, edited by Ananya Roy and Nezar AlSayyad. Lanham, MD.: Lexington Books, 2004.

Altvater, Elmar. "Globalization and the Informalization of Urban Space." In *Informal City: Caracas Case*, edited by Alfredo Brillembourg, Kristin Feiress and Hubert Klumpner. Munich: Prestel Verlag, 2005.

Appadurai, Arjun. "Deep Democracy: Urban Governmentality and the Horizon of Politics." *Public Culture* 14.1 (2002): 21-47.

Bayat, Asef. "From 'Dangerous Classes' to 'Quiet Rebels': Politics of the Urban Subaltern in the Global South." *International Sociology* 15.3 (2000): 533-557.

Benton, Lauren A., Manuel Castells and Alejandro Portes, eds. *The Informal Economy: Studies in Advanced and Less Developed Economies*. Baltimore, MD.: Johns Hopkins University Press, 1989.

Brand, Stewart. "How Slums Can Save the Planet." *Prospect* (February 2010). 39-41.

Castells, Manuel. "Why the Mega-cities Focus?" *The Mega-Cities Project Publication* MCP-018 (1998).

Cruz, Teddy "Trans-border Flows: An Urbanism Beyond the Property Line." In *Urban Transformation*, edited by Ilka Ruby and Andreas Ruby. Berlin: Ruby Press, 2008.

De Soto, Hernando. *The Mystery of Capital*. London: Black Swan, 2001.

Franck, Karen and Quentin Stevens, eds. *Loose Space: Possibility and Diversity in Urban Life*. London: Routledge, 2006.

Frug, Gerald. "A 'Rule of Law' for Cities." *Urban Age Mumbai Newspaper Essay*, 2007. Accessed January 17, 2012. http://www.urban-age.net/0_downloads/archive/_mumbai/Newspaper-essays_Frug.pdf.

Gandy, Matthew. "Learning from Lagos." *New Left Review* 33 (2005): 36-52.

Harvey, David "The Right to the City." *New Left Review* 53 (2008): 23-40.

Koolhaas, Rem. "Whatever Happened to Urbanism?" In *S,M,L,XL*, edited by Rem Koolhaas and Bruce Mau. New York: The Monicelli Press, 1995.

Misselwitz, Philipp, Philipp Oswalt, and Klaus Overmayer, eds. *Urban Catalyst: Strategies for Temporary Use.* Barcelona: Actar, 2009

Neuwirth, Robert. "Squatters and the Cities of Tomorrow." *City* 11.1 (2007): 71-80.

Perlman, Janice. *The Myth of Marginality: Urban Poverty and Politics in Rio de Janeiro.* Berkeley, CA.: University of California Press, 1976.

Roy, Ananya. "Strangely Familiar: Planning and the Worlds of Insurgence and Informality." *Planning Theory* 8.1 (2009): 7-11.

——. "Transnational Trespassing: The Geopolitics of Urban Informality." In *Urban Informality: Transnational Perspectives from the Middle East, Latin America, and South Asia*, edited by Ananya Roy and Nezar AlSayyad. Lanham, MD.: Lexington Books, 2004.

——. "The Gentleman's City: Urban Informality in the Calcutta of the New Communism." In *Urban Informality: Transnational Perspectives from the Middle East, Latin America, and South Asia*, edited by Ananya Roy and Nezar AlSayyad. Lanham: Lexington Books, 2004.

Sanyal, Romola. "Squatting in Camps: Building and Insurgency in Spaces of Refuge." *Urban Studies* 48.5 (2011): 877–890.

Sennett, Richard. *The Uses of Disorder: Personal Identity and City Life.* New York: Knopf, 1970.

Simone, Abdoumaliq. *For the City Yet to Come: Changing African Life in Four Cities.* Durham, NC.: Duke University Press, 2004.

Turner, John. *Housing by People: Towards Autonomy in Building Environments.* London: Marion Boyars, 1976.

Unruh, Jon D. "Debates: Urbanization in the Developing World and the Acutely Tenure Insecure." *City* 11.1 (2007): 115-120.

WWF. *Social Platform Through Social Innovations: A Coalition with Women in the Informal Sector.* Chennai: Working Women's Forum, 2000.

Yiftachel, Oren. "Theoretical Notes on 'Gray Cities': The Coming of Urban Apartheid?" *Planning Theory* 8.1 (2009): 88–100.

A Wild Rich villa in Belgrade's Padina, a neighborhood that grew rapidly with the influx of approximately 1,500 wealthy families in the period between 1995 and 2005.

Brick and Gold: The Urbanism and Architecture of Informal Belgrade

By
Milica Topalović

Normality

"A perfectly normal city" were the words incidentally over-
heard by a small German art collective on the streets of
Belgrade during the early days of 1996. Its members had
traveled to Belgrade to participate in one of the many unofficial cultural gatherings organized by the urban left that
had been stirring a critical voice in the city. Only halfway
through the Yugoslav crisis—and at a time of international
sanctions, the politicization of everyday life, obsessive
propaganda, and the complete shift of state and city functions into informality and the "Wild City"—the description
of Belgrade as "perfectly normal" expressed an important
insight. The half-poignant, half-resigned realization sug-
gested that the anomaly of Belgrade's urban condition
had become so pervasive and thorough that it had actually
reached a critical point, from which it had begun to install
itself as a new kind of normality.

Several years later, Belgrade's ability to turn an anomaly into normality and informal activity into a norm had become so established that it was on the verge of becoming an international brand. In 2003, Rem Koolhaas paid a working visit to the Serbian Ministry of Culture. Though somewhat overshadowed by the attention paid to his public appearance, the visit served the aim of discussing how the post-socialist capital and country could redefine their compromised identities (in the context of a possible commission for their redesign). Koolhaas adviced Belgrade not to emulate a Western European capital—as it would inevitably only amount to a B or C-rated version of the original—but to instead capitalize on its preeminent capacity for lowering urban standards, which it could offer as a service to cities with higher standards than necessary.[1]

While roughly illustrating Belgrade's experience of stabilizing the informal, this brief anecdote points in several directions. As Koolhaas' discussion with the Serbian ministry was without any real consequence, it is fair to assume that the country's federal and municipal officials were not quite sure what to do with the proffered advice. Their actual role in the urban sphere had, after all, been reduced to facilitating a decision-making process between traditional and newly formed political and economic actors. Tangled up in transitional administrations with overlapping responsibilities and conflicting interests, they often contradicted themselves, too. If in the end they helped fuel the growing informalization of the city, this was neither as a follow up to Koolhaas' suggestion nor the implementation of any established policy, but the consequence of their sheer inability to act. Looking at the physical space of the city, the wild, improvised, and informal development that occurred during this transitional period was perhaps Belgrade's only successful urban practice from that time. The two-hundred thousand informal structures built since 1990 produced a shift in scale in the city's urban landscape and an abun-

1 Srdjan Jovanović Weiss, "Belgrade: Where Subversion is Normal," *Perspecta* 39 (2007): 49–57.

dant collection of new urban typologies, which, while not complying with regulations, are both consolidated and functional. From Koolhaas' optimistic vantage point, the city's ability to "lower urban standards" could prominently position Belgrade as a candidate for European integration.

In the urban domain, the transfer of state and municipal responsibility from formal structures to informal networks—a process that started slowly under socialism in the sixties and escalated during the crisis of the nineties—eventually came to be driven by far more than the urgent necessity to maintain the city's vital functions. In the period extending from before Slobodan Milošević's fall from power in 2000 to the present, informality has proven to be cheaper, faster, and more stable and efficient than previous socio-political configurations. Informal operations have a strong tendency to progress: The micro-interventions that addressed the individual need for housing and jobs, characteristic of the early stages of the crisis in the 1990s, have been gradually replaced by developments of higher standards. With both the public and private sector contributing to informal networks, as well as the citizenry, although often by no choice of their own, Belgrade has moved well beyond the crisis to an unprecedented state of urban stability outside of law and urban planning.

Origin and Growth

Spontaneous and unregulated construction had little relevance in Belgrade during the nineteenth- and early twentieth-century, even though the construction of second homes for the wealthy on the forested hillsides of Senjak and Dedinje was rarely regulated or permitted. Informality only became an important phenomenon in the middle of the twentieth century, when it emerged either as a tolerated or overlooked supplement to modern city planning. Relations between municipal authorities and the protagonists of informality transformed from complete non-toleration under socialism to the full permissiveness experienced in

■■ City center

■■ Old suburbs and modern extensions

■ Informal settlements and satellite towns

Fig. 1. Distribution of illegal buildings in Belgrade.

more recent times. Under socialism, informal construction gradually intensified, though limited to housing. This began in the early fifties and continued into the seventies, with a steady influx of migrants from the rural areas exceeding the pace of housing construction in the city. The squats in the common spaces of New Belgrade's mega-blocks and the informal settlements on the city's periphery became the norm rather than the exception. Against this reality, socialist "parade urbanism," as it was later coined, provided for only the advantaged population, which was enough for a rhetorical endorsement of the socialist housing policy.

The embargo imposed by the United Nations in 1992 helped distribute informal energy far beyond the production of housing. Half of the city's population is thought to have built or ran a business illegally, compensating for diminished public and financial sector services with activities such as informal public transport, gasoline trade, and street commerce. Under the pressure of an economic crisis and the hyperinflation of the early nineties, state-owned housing stock was privatized and the profits transferred elsewhere. Housing production subsequently became an individual concern. Milošević's government displayed no interest in recapturing institutional influence, leaving impoverished municipal authorities with no choice but to generate income informally on their own turf. Public parking lots and parks, for example, were rented out to shops and kiosks—a practice that was based on a system of temporary building permissions that suspended all rules in favor of maximizing profits.

Since 2000, and with the partial normalization of the political system, informal structures and networks have tended to stabilize and achieve legality through open negotiations with its formal counterparts, shifting power and responsibility into the private sphere. Several other important characteristics can be linked to this transformation. Architecturally, the informal city is in the process of consolidating. Helped by a growing indifference in society at large, step-by-step additions have turned the myriad

Stages of the informalization process in the housing sector:

Fig 2.1: Before World War II: Precursors. Farms on the perimeter of Belgrade provided the nucleus for informal suburbs.

Fig 2.2: 1960s to 1980s: Socialist informalism. Self-constructed migrant housing on the periphery was tolerated under socialism.

Fig 2.3: 1980s and early 1990s: Redbrick era. Working-class informal settlements built of red brick boomed in the eighties and proliferated during the nineties, becoming the largest section of informal Belgrade.

Fig 2.4: The "Wild Rich" era. New elites began building informally,
with corruption, money laundering, and old boys' networks as driving forces.

Fig 2.5: Informal developers. Since law enforcement and hence demolition
was increasingly unlikely, the scale of informal operations grew.
New developers sold apartments on the informal market, quickly transferring
the risks of illegality to their clients.

Fig 2.6: Stabilization. Recent informal buildings display a confidence similar to that of developments in regulated European situations. A kind of typological and rhetorical normalization emerges. Illegal or semi-legal apartment buildings can generate a profit of two-hundred to three-hundred percent.

of provisional and mobile objects (kiosks, stands, goods displayed on boxes and car hoods) that emerged in the early nineties into matter-of-fact typologies backed by legal papers. At the same time, the scale of interventions and investments has increased, with individual wild builders replaced by informal developers. Socially, this is a process of segmentation that involves the rise of new hierarchies; only the initial phase is relatively anarchic.

After 2000, the authorities sought to bring order to the chaos, addressing both the physical impact of the illegal city and the various informal practices still prevalent. One serious obstacle has been the widespread distrust felt toward the government. For instance, the "Social Assessment of Serbia," a draft by the World Bank, reported that with the exception of the church, army, and police, state institutions are trusted by less than ten percent of the population.

At the same time, in the years following Serbia's transition to democracy in 2000, the informal energy of individual citizens also fell out of focus. Institutional attention turned instead to public land formerly owned by the Socialist state, which was opened up to private investors in order to accelerate the privatization of the city's assets.

The Periphery

Bewilderingly, the informal periphery of Belgrade is strikingly similar to a Western single-family suburb. Nothing about it is precarious; instead, it is peaceful, normal, even well off. The sensation is nevertheless puzzling and the similarity is both alienating and uncanny. At a second glance, differences begin to reveal themselves, unveiling what looks like a carefully orchestrated subversion.

Houses are large and affluent. They appear unfinished, even though the neighborhood looks like it has been settled for quite a while. Building volumes give an impression of homogeneity and sameness, but a closer look yields no in-

Fig. 3: An informal neighborhood in the south of Belgrade.

tentional repetition of details, elements, or geometric forms.

Streets are quiet and pedestrian-friendly, and, yet, there are no sidewalks. In fact, the entire bandwidth of regular street design elements is missing: there are no strips of greenery, bicycle paths, parking lots, demarcated traffic lanes, concrete curbs, raised or lowered surfaces. All that exists is a street, which, like a narrow gutter, winds between the houses, sometimes quite beautifully.

The surface of the terrain, a former field, is clearly visible and stretches continuously beneath the buildings, uninterrupted and unaltered. Without precisely balanced poles of activity, like a front and back, gardens appear as neutral green carpets on which houses are simply and somewhat haphazardly placed.

No design—urban, architectural, or otherwise—situates the neighborhood and its residents within a specific cultural or aesthetic milieu. The wild suburb does not reproduce or evoke any known urban or suburban model; neither a garden city nor cul-de-sac, or even a village, the neighborhood replicates nothing other than itself. No prevalent cultural themes are invoked here, not even the desire for a home of one's own. Identity is generic and conforming—even individualized expressions quickly blend into a recognizable and predictable murmur of references where local, rural, folk, neo-folk, and (some say) themes and traditions from telenovelas dominate.

If Western suburbs demonstrate a desire to leave the city behind, informal suburbs demonstrate the inverse: a desire to stay as close to it as possible. The informal belt of Belgrade points toward the city center. Its force is strongly centripetal.

If there's inventiveness somewhere in the informal city, it's located in the design of these suburbs and their meticulous reductions, which affect standards, regulations, participants, urban and architectural elements, and, ultimately, the materiality and perception of space. The informal city is the triumphant absence of the suburb as we know it; and, yet, it is almost perfectly contrived.

Land

Informal construction never starts from a tabula rasa;
there is always either a pretext or alibi and usually it's
that of unsettled land rights. Although disputes over land
ownership in Belgrade are often apologetically backdated
to as far back as the Ottoman and Habsburg rule, present
problems mainly developed during the socialist nationaliza-
tion of land in 1945 and its denationalization in the early
1990s.[2]

Located on the outskirts of Belgrade, the development
of Padina is a perfect example of the genesis of an informal
district. Ever since the Second World War, agricultural land
has been steadily sold in Padina for residential development. In recent years, this process has escalated to the
point where all private agricultural land in the city is said
to have been subdivided and sold as pseudo-plots, which
are now circulating in the informal land market, only at
much higher prices. In Belgrade, the construction of private
homes on formerly agricultural land constitutes a clas-
sic example of illegal construction and is viewed relatively
benignly as a result of necessity. The occupation of publicly
or privately owned land—parks, forests, sports fields,
sidewalks, landslide terrains, waste disposal sites, and
infrastructure corridors—is considered a much more problematic and dangerous category of appropriation. State
authorities, including the military, have also developed
their own properties for profit or political advantage by, for
example, subdividing the land of formerly state-owned agricultural estates, *kombinati*, to house refugees from the war
zones of former Yugoslavia. At times, the frenzy to occupy a

2 Denationalization is seen as a major obstacle to privatization and clarifying
property relations on building land. One of the first steps to denationalize
property took place in 1992, when publicly owned agrarian land was returned
to its former private owners. The act was labelled by the opposition as an
election treat from Milošević to the people. A general denationalization of land
and real estate has not yet taken place, with the exception of the so-called
special categories of owners, which includes the Serbian Orthodox church.
For more information, see the Directorate for Restitution of the Republic of
Serbia, http://www.restitucija.gov.rs/?lang=en.

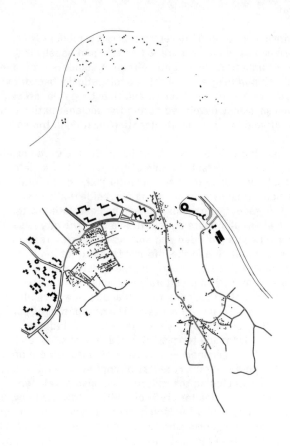

Fig. 4: The genesis and growth of an informal settlement: Padina.

Top, 1930s: Agricultural settlement: The first record of Padina and its
small number of agricultural households dates back to 1937.
Bottom, 1980s: Village structure: Padina remained a village until the eighties,
with some early informal houses built during the socialist period. In the mid-
eighties, the infrastructure for the housing development Braće Jerković II was
completed to the north of Padina, connecting the village to the city center.

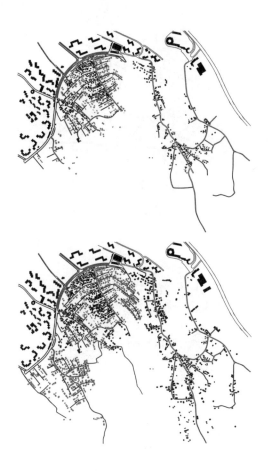

Top, 1990s: The Wild Rich: The many affluent newcomers to Padina built dwellings at a high standard for themselves. The old village structure was altered
by extensions to existing buildings. The new middle class of Padina consisted
primarily of refugees who constructed simple homes for their extended families.
Bottom, 1995–2005: Although the master plan for Padina (Municipalities of
Zvezdara and Voždovac, an area of two-hundred hectares) tried to integrate
existing informal structures ex post facto, as it were, because of corruption it
had to be updated annually to accommodate the latest illegal developments in
the area.

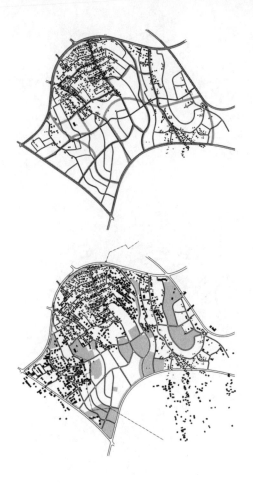

The post-factum revision of plans is most evident in the planning of streets and public amenities. Placed side by side, plans from 1995 and 2005 show that compromises were also made with regard to individual buildings.

Top: Building stock around 1995, street planning in 1997, and adapted street network in 2005. Bottom: Building stock in 2005, planned public spaces in 2005.

plot of one's own reached epic proportions as both air and water rights were colonized in addition to land rights. With no clear ownership rules and good infrastructure to plug into, roofs are a bonus, while dense water plots along the banks of the Sava and Danube River provide attractive options in which property questions are entirely bypassed.

Recent attempts to resolve the complex issue of land rights in informal settlements—by tracing the land's original owners, for example, or retroactively reparcelling the land and rezoning—have generally been fruitless. Throughout the past decade, such legalization procedures have had the paradoxical effect of stimulating further informal construction and causing land prices to rise even higher. Moreover, the impossibility of taxation combined with a lack of funds has blocked any effort to rehabilitate neighborhoods; recovering private land in informal neighborhoods for the construction of public facilities, such as schools, can take years.

Nevertheless, the situation has its potentials. The rapid occupation of land on a first come, first served basis has produced areas that seem immune to the segregation patterns of lifestyle and income. Under conditions of unexpected proximity and high density, farms neighbor redbrick houses, just as marble mansions neighbor illegal apartment buildings.[3] Belgrade's Wild Rich, farmers, and paupers live right next to each other in a relaxed configuration that makes informal urbanism look like a successful social project.

Backbones

The conceptual gulf between the unstable collectivism of the sixties and seventies and the ethos of self-realization of the nineties corresponds to a physical demarcation of space that that is easily discerned in Belgrade and could

3 Zoran Žegarac, "Illegal Construction in Belgrade and the Prospects for Urban Development Planning," *Cities* 16.5 (1999): 365–370.

Fig. 5: A roundabout on Ustanička Ulica on the edge of Konjarnik, a modern neighborhood, with the Eastern Gate of Belgrade in the background.

be represented in a map. This space, which links redbrick belts to modern extensions in the city, consists only of infrastructure. Built as arterial roads to carry socialist workers swiftly and smoothly from the center to their high-rise apartments on the periphery, from where they could admire an unspoiled landscape, these roads have today been converted into axes of provision. At once too ordinary and picturesque, the streets are lined with improvised businesses under red roof tiles, concrete towers, and gypsum villas. Along this inner frontier, end-of-the-line bus stops surrounded by kiosks stand like gates to the planned city.

Infrastructures

As infrastructure becomes increasingly localized, the days of totalizing networks are over. Looking across the edge of Belgrade's modern periphery, an unsurprising contrast manifests itself: Here, an organic and irregular urban fabric emerges out of regular street grids and regional roads.

The modern infrastructures inherited from socialism have been treated as a source of public revenue, which has caused a great deal of controversy. New infrastructure is only built selectively at highly visible and politically sensitive locations such as the airport, New Belgrade's central zone, the Prokop and Vukov Spomenik railway stations, and on the riverbanks.

In the city's distant fringes, infrastructure is also instrumentalized to manage informal construction. The meeting points of public and private infrastructure are easily recognized as places where streets suddenly shrink, sidewalks vanish, and massive tangles of cables hang in the air; the desire to control meets the desire for autonomy here, and the urban domain breaks up into a capsular world. In its attempts to regain control, the Serbian government permitted informal builders to link up to the electricity network, with a silent and clearly political approval given behind the urbanists' backs. Nevertheless, residents of informal neighborhoods self-organized to assert their local

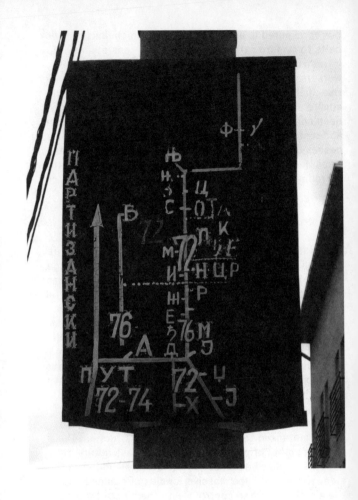

Fig. 6: Street numbers such as "72p" recall the informal subdivision of land, Karaburma district.

independence and began to build missing infrastructures by themselves. They determined addresses, street names, and numbers, which the postal service is flexible enough to deliver to. In Padina, street names are pragmatic, spelling out "Entry 1," "Entry 2," "Entry n," while in Kaludjerica, Belgrade's largest informal settlement, names are copied from the city center or taken from the hometowns of refugees. In Karaburma, the number of houses at a single legal address is limited only by the number of letters in the Cyrillic alphabet.

Though many of Belgrade's informal neighborhoods are moving toward standards closer to those of the city center, self-organization also has its limits. As more and more illegal mansions in Padina plug into communal plumbing networks, for example, self-made infrastructures are stretched to their breaking point, instilling a constant fear of complete paralysis. For the time being, however, crisis is a distant possibility: Belgrade's informal settlers feel secure in their gray legal status and satisfied with the living conditions that they have achieved, and revenue from illegal construction helps maintain this status quo.

Housing

Redundancy is the basic attribute of informal housing. In a city where building speculation is one of the few ways to make profit—especially during the crisis—assessing needs is a risky enterprise and supply easily exceeds demand. Serbia, including Belgrade, has both a declining and an aging population, coupled with a present industrial standstill. The current master plan predicts that between now and 2021, Belgrade will need an additional 50,000 houses—approximately the number of already existing illegal and semi-legal housing units built as speculative ventures in a city now stagnant.[4]

4 Miodrag Ferenčak, Director of General, Spatial, and Urbanistic Planning at the Town Planning Institute Belgrade, in conversation with Members of ETH Studio Basel, Belgrade, Serbia, April 2006.

It might come as a surprise that the projection has not been used as an argument against illegal construction; on the contrary, in this transitional stage, informal construction has become a factor in Serbia's social, economic, and, hence, political stability, even if it is redundant. Informal housing occupies the lower end of the housing market and forms a stable segment of its own. In this situation, legality is more a tool used to deliberately balance social and economic issues than an all-encompassing necessity. Throughout the transition period, informal construction has effectively amounted to an unofficial social policy, under the tacit assumption that "bricklaying and building many unnecessary houses is at least an engagement in a correct, creative activity."[5]

Permanently unfinished and always under construction define the aesthetic character of the informal dwelling, as well as the key feature of its economic success. In Belgrade, as elsewhere in Europe, mass production eagerly meets a do-it-yourself mentality in the housing market; developers deliver apartments in an intermediate stage and housing standards remain open for negotiation.

Building is spare-time work; for many, it represents quality leisure time. It is therefore not a surprise that informal neighborhoods look and feel like a weekday during the weekend—that is, like a huge construction site. With its latent anarchic energy, ceaseless construction is a culture, a social space, and, ultimately, a way of life.

Public Space

Throughout the era of wild expansion, a jungle-like quality dominated the country's broadcasting and telecommunication sector. During the nineties, as many as 1,500 radio and TV stations, with partial or temporary licenses or operating entirely as pirate outposts, were believed to have battled for on-air presence and stronger frequencies in Serbia. The

5 Ferenčak, in conversation with Members of ETH Studio Basel.

explosion in volume of this mediated public space was directly proportional to an escalating collective media obsession, fed by nationalist fervor, frontline news, and hypnotic turbo-folk rhythms. By contrast, Belgrade's physical public realm imploded, its authority dismissed, its place in the city progressively filled by rough-and-ready shops and grass-carpet cafés with sponsored umbrellas.

In Belgrade's informal settlements, public space is scarce. The few actors engaged in Belgrade's informal settlements, among them NGOs and citizens' groups, are more concerned with the improvement of public amenities and infrastructure than with public space. And, yet, the informal areas of Belgrade do not lack space, as there is plenty of redundant land: plots locked in speculation and failed investment, heaps of construction material, scattered carcasses of concrete foundations and floor slabs. Space is everywhere, but it is not public; instead, the city's informal settlements are pervaded by the residual.

Planning

A practice of making plans after the facts of construction emerged in Belgrade in the mid-nineties, by which point it was evident that informal construction was rapidly becoming mainstream. In place of demolition, which would have been both ineffecient and costly, the city's focus shifted to improving infrastructure and providing services and public transport. The individual examples of post-factum planning reveal the difficulties of this approach and Belgrade's Wild Rich Padina illustrates an almost satirical scenario. Between 1995 and 2005, the neighborhood boomed as approximately 1,500 wealthy families made it their home. The peculiar profile of Padina made it possible for newcomers to mobilize both bottom-up and top-down practices, as they had control over the land as well as considerable political influence. As a result, a bizarre negotiating process unfolded between the reality of the neighborhood's frenetic construction and a plan that continually lagged behind.

The builders operated tactically and kept close to the provisional outlines of their future legality, determining the building height, distances between buildings, and their position in the street according to the given plan. Meanwhile, at the planners' desk, political power and corruption helped integrate recent developments from Padina's construction sites, resulting in the publication of a continuous stream of updates.

The effects of this process soon began to crystallize in an inflationary form of planning: Design made a gradual exit as streets shriveled to organic zigzags and public spaces timidly migrated toward the edge of the settlement. With urban planning institutions lacking any operative authority, to plan in this case meant legitimizing Padina's rampant construction of informal villas, while giving up on urbanism.

Legalization

The legalization process initiated in Belgrade during the past decade has not been effective. Rather, it became an example of populist political strategies that make it less expensive to legalize illegal constructions than to build legally from the start. (For instance, the legalization process required illegal homeowners to hire architects to retroactively document the construction. A quick calculation of the time needed to document Belgrade's 200,000 illegal buildings suggests that this would provide full employment for an entire generation of graduates from the Belgrade Faculty of Architecture, i.e. roughly a hundred architects.) With 200,000 to 300,000 informal builders in Belgrade and more than 150,000 requests for legalization, the legal status has been a political trade-off.[6] Instead of yielding expected benefits like clarity, tax revenue, reliable data, security, and effective planning, the legalization procedure

6 Dragan Krsnik, "Opet cveta divlja gradnja," *Večernje Novosti*, March 22, 2009, accessed February 8, 2011, http://www.novosti.rs/vesti/beograd.74. html:235104-Opet-cveta-divlja-gradnja.

has been hampered by unclear land ownership, missing documentation, and overburdened institutions.

Underscoring the Darwinian qualities of the informal city, most smaller structures that qualify for the legalization process, like family dwellings, have been caught in a bureaucratic deadlock, while powerful informal developers continue to operate above the law. A piece of legislation from 2003 that meant to bring about a general end to illegal construction instead opened up a new field of possibilities for illegal but nonetheless realizable construction.[7] Investors in legal structures have even protested their perceived discrimination, as wild construction in the suburbs continues to flourish under the cover of applying for legalization. The entire procedure of obtaining a building permit has become senseless in the context of post-factum building licenses, which provide an easier and cheaper alternative to construction.

With the social, political, and economic benefits of informal construction outweighing its hazards, legality and illegality have coexisted as two equally useful options. The value of legality is calculated in view of a future incorporation into the EU; but, as an option, it remains expensive, complex, and difficult, if not even completely impossible. The value of established and ordered illegality, in turn, is based on and backed by constant investment in networks that have proven more stable than transitional governmental frameworks.

Efficiency

Compared to construction that meets European standards and that involves investors, urban planners, architects and designers, bankers, city authorities, users, and developers, Belgrade's informal development schemes, in which regulations are provisional, and design, credits, and professional

---

7 "Zakon o planiranju i izgradnji," *Službeni Glasnik Republike Srbije* 47 (2003).

Efficiency of legal and illegal building processes:

Fig. 7.1: A legal building process: After a plot of land is purchased legally from a dealer, the developer has to wait two years for a building permit. Construction is professional and finished within a year. Apartments are sold at 1,000 € per square meter, generating a high level of returns. The whole process from land purchase to delivery to the buyer takes approximately three years. Padina, 2006.

Fig 7.2: An illegal building process: A plot of land is purchased illegally from a farmer and developed by a family, often working together with friends. The price of the house reaches 450 € per square meter. The house will most likely be legalized in the future at a fee of 30 € per square meter. Infrastructure is acquired legally. The construction process takes a year and a half before a family can move in. The expected returns are at two hundred to three hundred percent. Padina, 2006.

construction, unnecessary, are surprisingly more efficient. Stabilized within a market, planning process, and legal framework, its efficiency is based on economic rationality: Building illegally in Belgrade can be as much as four times as cheap as its legal counterpart and construction time is cut in half. In addition, adherence to regulations promises unparalleled benefits through security against demolition. Illegality is cheaper, faster, and, altogether, not a great risk, which makes it very attractive. When compared with housing markets in European countries, informal Belgrade always wins.

Metaphors

The banality of Belgrade's informal buildings stands in sharp contrast to the expectations that architecture academia has long had of informalism. The accelerated growth of informal cities all over the world during the fifties and sixties served as a fountain of inspiration for counter streams to the Modern Movement that emerged at the time. A growing fascination with regionalism and the vernacular, spontaneous, and ordinary can be found in the work of groups and individuals as diverse as Team X, the Situationists, and Christopher Alexander. In the early seventies, the concepts of informality and self-organization were introduced in economics and in the realm of physics and complex systems. Today, the proliferation of computational design tools has brought similar interests back into the architectural context, along with a new set of natural metaphors and techniques, such as swarm intelligence and artificial life. Though such research has been applied in many fields, it has not yet touched upon the actual physical space of informal cities—a space that, according to the UN, constitutes a third of our urbanized world.

Numerous assumptions are built into these metaphorical interpretations: first and foremost, that computational tools can be predictive; secondly, that the ability of bottom-up systems to generate innovation is far beyond that of top-down designers; and, finally, that citizens who build their own environments and communities engage in a process of political emancipation.

While the first assumption—that we can predict informal growth—may be of interest for statistics, it is hardly relevant for the scale and morphology of cities like Belgrade, where processes are too rapid and fragmented to conform to any general and predictable patterns.

The second assumption, as applied to innovation in Belgrade's informal architecture, is partially valid. It is true that informal construction brought Belgrade its first genuine house-on-skyscraper parasite and house-in-kiosk hybrid, as well as a bus stop on a highway, but beyond this hopeful collection of ready-mades, the creativity of Belgrade's informal architecture is strongest in its ability to tactically maneuver in the legal field, calculated in terms of stretching its limits. The tactics at work here are numerous and generate forms able to anticipate future laws and regulations. The forms might defy laws and regulation (through an appearance of power or the power of multitude), conform to them (through a markedly normal look), camouflage excess (e.g. many extra floors), or seek alibis (by extending in all directions around parts of structures that have permits)—but they always stay close to that which is or can become legal. The ability to negotiate with the law is a special gift of Belgrade's informal architecture. In staying close to conventions, and displaying a wish for permanence, acknowledgment, and a more ordered future, its normalcy is inventive, too.

The third assumption—of emancipation and the gradual emergence of a legitimate and critical political voice through an informal process—does not hold in Belgrade. In fact, the opposite has been the case: The informal energy in the city was quickly channeled into official political interests, such as refugee settlement, voter reliance, and economic and social benefits. A certain degree of formalization of informal groups and organized pressure against the government does exist, however, and groups such as the Association of Street Vendors and the Association of

Informal Home Owners have turned to the streets and the press to demand support and acknowledgment. Kaludjerica—the largest informal settlement in Europe and the oldest in Belgrade, with 80,000 houses built following the Kosovo crisis in the early eighties—is the foremost example of an informal situation. Kaludjerica does not have a local government, nor does it campaign for municipal autonomy, but it does have its own website with printable maps for visitors, just like any other suburban town in Europe—heralding a sort of high renaissance of the informal sphere.

European City

Where does Belgrade's situation position the city within the European framework? Can Belgrade contribute to a new understanding of informalism in Europe? Is informal Belgrade even a European city? Relatively removed from the problems of the crisis-prone cities of the so-called Third World, the West has a long history of romanticizing the informal. Looking from Belgrade toward a post social-democratic Western Europe, it is clear that parallels between the city's informalism and Europe's neoliberal denationalization have long been obscured and downplayed. When the crisis first erupted in Belgrade and Serbia, the general perception was that its wildness was locally specific, like a pathological reaction to war and embargos; but eventually, its links with Western deregulation became more apparent. However, the driving forces behind these converging processes originate from entirely different motives. In the mid-nineties, Belgrade's frenzied informal construction reacted to the breakdown of state planning and construction. Meanwhile, in the West, a more moderate and desirable wildness was promoted in a neoromantic claim for individualization. In the Netherlands, for example, Carl Weeber's *Het Wilde Wonen* (translated as "Wild Living" or "Desired Living") proposed in 1998 a major initiative for the reform of spatial planning and housing policy. Hailed as "the abandonment of state planning in architecture" (and of the moralizing tendencies of the seventies and eighties, as represented by the Dutch architects Aldo van Eyck, Herman Herzberger, and their respective generations), this new housing ideal was a product of the ongoing liberalization of the housing market—an opportunity for "fewer rules and more individual freedom," in which "people themselves compose or build their own homes."[8]

What does the future hold for informal Belgrade? Will architects and urbanists eventually return to the Wild City? And when and if they do, will they play the role of state bureaucrats, social actors, or perhaps that of stars? For the moment everything is possible and nothing is predictable. But one thing is certain: As it leaves the borderlines of Europe for the mainstream, Belgrade is and has always been a perfectly normal city.

This text is an excerpt from an essay "Brick and Gold: The Urbanism and Architecture of Informal Belgrade," originally published in ETH Studio Basel, *Belgrade – Formal / Informal: A Research on Urban Transformation* (Zürich: Verlag Scheidegger & Spiess, 2011).

Bibliography:

Ferenčak, Miodrag. In conversation with Members of ETH Studio Basel. Belgrade, Serbia. April 2006.

Jovanović Weiss, Srdjan. "Belgrade: Where Subversion is Normal." *Perspecta* 39 (2007): 49–57.

Krsnik, Dragan. "Opet cveta divlja gradnja." *Večernje Novosti*. March 22, 2009. Accessed February 8, 2011. http://www.novosti.rs/vesti/beograd.74. html:235104-Opet-cveta-divlja-gradnja.

Weeber, Carel and Wouter Vanstiphout. *Het Wilde Wonen*. Rotterdam: 010 publishers, 1998.

"Zakon o planiranju i izgradnji." *Službeni Glasnik Republike Srbije* 47 (2003).

Žegarac, Zoran, "Illegal Construction in Belgrade and the Prospects for Urban Development Planning." *Cities* 16.5 (1999): 365–370.

8 Carel Weeber and Wouter Vanstiphout, *Het Wilde Wonen* (Rotterdam: 010 publishers, 1998).

I. AM. NOT. A. SLUMDO[G]

I AM THE FUTURE OF INDI[A]

Residents from the slums of Mumbai protest the use of the word "dog" in the title of the blockbuster movie *Slumdog Millionaire*, waving signs that say, "We slumdwellers are humans and not dogs," 2009.

Slumdog Cities: Rethinking Subaltern Urbanism

By Ananya Roy

"Across a filthy, rubbish-filled creek we enter the slum's heaving residential area, treading carefully to ensure we do not step in human sewage. Live wires hang from wobbly walls; we crouch through corridor-like passages between houses made from reclaimed rubble as the sky disappears above our heads. Behind flimsy doorway curtains we spy babies sleeping on dirty mattresses in tiny single room homes, mothers busy washing, cooking and cleaning. The few hours I spend touring Mumbai's teeming Dharavi slum are uncomfortable and upsetting, teetering on voyeuristic. They are also among the most uplifting of my life. Instead of a neighbourhood characterised by misery, I find a bustling and enterprising place, packed with small-scale industries defying their circumstances to flourish amidst the squalor. Rather than pity, I am inspired by man's alchemic ability to thrive when the chips are down."[1]

Simon Crerar, 2010

1 Simon Crerar, "Mumbai Slum Tour: Why You Should See Dharavi," *Times*, May 13, 2010, accessed June 10, 2010, http://www.timesonline.co.uk/tol/travel/destinations/india/article7124205.ece.

"Postcolonial studies, unwittingly commemorating a lost object, can become an alibi unless it is placed within a general frame."[2]

Gayatri Chakravorty Spivak, 1999

In the urban imagination of the new millennium, the megacity has become shorthand for the human condition of the Global South. Cities of enormous size, they are delineated through what Jennifer Robinson has called "developmentalism."[3] Their herculean problems of underdevelopment—poverty, environmental toxicity, disease—are the grounds for numerous diagnostic and reformist interventions. The megacity can therefore be understood as the "constitutive outside" of contemporary urban studies, existing in a relationship of difference with the dominant norm of the global city—urban nodes that are seen to be command and control points of the world economy. Following Chantal Mouffe, who in turn relies on Jacques Derrida, the "constitutive outside" is not a dialectical opposite but rather a condition of emergence, an outside that by being inside creates "radical undecidability."[4] The megacity thus renders the very category of global city impossible, revealing the limits, porosities, and fragilities of all global centers. Is there a megacity future for every global city? What global city can function without relational dependence on seemingly distant economies of fossil fuels and cheap labor? In this sense, the megacity marks the limits of archival and ethnographic recognition. In this sense, the megacity is the *subaltern* of urban studies. It cannot be represented in the archives of knowledge and it cannot therefore be the subject of history.

2 Gayatri Chakravorty Spivak, *A Critique of Postcolonial Reason: Toward a History of the Vanishing Present* (Cambridge, MA: Harvard University Press, 1999), 1.
3 Jennifer Robinson, "Global and World Cities: A View from Off the Map," *International Journal of Urban and Regional Research* 26.3 (2002): 531.
4 Chantal Mouffe, *The Democratic Paradox* (New York: Verso, 2000), 12.

This article is an intervention in the epistemologies and methodologies of urban studies. In it, I seek to understand and transform the ways in which the cities of the Global South are studied and represented in urban research and to some extent in popular discourse. As such, the article is primarily concerned with a formation of ideas—*subaltern urbanism*—which undertakes the theorization of the megacity and its subaltern spaces and subaltern classes. Of these, the ubiquitous "slum" is the most prominent. Writing against apocalyptic and dystopian narratives of the slum, subaltern urbanism provides accounts of the slum as a terrain of habitation, livelihood, and politics. This is a vital and even radical challenge to dominant narratives of the megacity. Subaltern urbanism then is an important paradigm, for it seeks to confer recognition on spaces of poverty and forms of popular agency that often remain invisible and neglected in the archives and annals of urban theory.

However, in this article I undertake a study of the limits of such itineraries of recognition by rethinking subaltern urbanism. Drawing on postcolonial theory, I shift the meaning of subaltern from the study of spaces of poverty and forms of popular agency to an interrogation of epistemological categories. Following the work of Gayatri Chakravorty Spivak, the subaltern can be understood as marking the limits of archival and ethnographic recognition; it is that which forces an analysis of dominant epistemologies and methodologies.[5] Meant to be more than an epistemological disruption, the article highlights emergent analytical strategies of research. In particular, four categories are discussed—peripheries, urban informality, zones of exception, and gray spaces. Informed by the urbanism of the Global South, these categories break with ontological and topological understandings of subaltern subjects and subaltern spaces.

5 Spivak, *A Critique of Postcolonial Reason.*

The Metonymic Slum

The megacity is a metonym for underdevelopment, Third Worldism, the Global South. As a metonym, the megacity conjures up an abject but uplifting human condition, one that lives in filth and sewage but is animated by the "alchemic ability" to survive and thrive.[6] And it is the slum, the Third World slum, that constitutes the iconic geography of this urban and human condition. It is the "recognizable frame" through which the cities of the Global South are perceived and understood, their difference mapped and located.[7] Much more is at stake here than Alan Gilbert's fear of the use of "an old, never euphemistic ... dangerous stereotype."[8] If we are to pay attention to what postcolonial critic Spivak has identified as the "worlding of what is now called the Third World," then it is necessary to confront how the megacity is worlded through the icon of the slum.[9] In other words, the slum has become the most common itinerary through which the Third World city (i.e. the megacity) is recognized.

I do not use the term "itinerary" casually. Today, the Third World slum is an itinerary, a "touristic transit."[10] The most obvious example of this is the slum tour, available in the Rocinha favela of Rio de Janeiro, the Soweto township of Johannesburg, the kampungs of Jakarta, and the Dharavi slum of Mumbai. One such slum itinerary appears epigraphically as the introduction to this article. In it, the *Times* journalist Simon Crerar introduces his readership to the "harsh existence of Mumbai's poor," but also to "spirit and enterprise," where the "pace of work" amidst "buzz-

6 Crerar, "Mumbai Slum Tour."
7 Sarah Nuttall and Achille Mbembe, "A Blasé Attitude: A Response to Michael Watts," *Public Culture* 17.1 (2005): 193.
8 Alan Gilbert, "The Return of the Slum: Does Language Matter?" *International Journal of Urban and Regional Research* 31.4 (2007): 701.
9 Gayatri Chakravorty Spivak, "Three Women's Texts and a Critique of Imperialism," *Critical Inquiry* 12.1 (1985): 262.
10 Bianca Freire-Medeiros, "The Favela and Its Touristic Transits," *Geoforum* 40.4 (2009): 580–588.

ing flies" is "breathtaking."[11] From plastic recyclers to the makers of poppadams, Crerar charts his itinerary of a humming and thriving slum. It is in keeping with the ethos of Reality Tours, the "ethical tourism" agency whose guides lead tours of Dharavi. Reality Tours presents Dharavi, "Asia's biggest 'slum,' as 'a place of poverty and hardship but also a place of enterprise, humour and non-stop activity.'"[12] Proud to be featured in travel guides ranging from *Frommer's* to *Lonely Planet*, Reality Tours make the claim that "Dharavi is the heart of small scale industries in Mumbai" with an "annual turnover of approximately US $665 million."[13] Tour profits are directed towards a non-profit organization that operates a school for slum children, and slum tourists are discouraged from wielding cameras and photographing slum reality.

Crerar's recent "slum and sightseeing tour" references two dramatic worldings of Mumbai: the "terrorist" attacks of November 2008 with its killing sites of luxury hotels and urban cafés and the blockbuster film *Slumdog Millionaire*. Indeed, Crerar's narrative begins with what is already a well-worn cliché: "I've wanted to visit Mumbai since Danny Boyle's *Slumdog Millionaire* swept to Oscar glory. The film is set in Dharavi, the dusty creek-bed where one million souls live in an area the size of London's Hyde Park, surrounded on all sides by Asia's most expensive real estate."[14] In *Slumdog Millionaire*, the various slums of Mumbai are combined into a singular composition that has come to be interpreted as Dharavi, Asia's largest slum. This too is a metonym—Dharavi: Slum.

Slumdog Millionaire is a worlding of the megacity, and of the metonymic megacity Mumbai. The film, with its story of a young slum-dweller and his dreams and aspiration, has been the focus of protests in India for both its apocalyptic

11 Crerar, "Mumbai Slum Tour."
12 "Reality Tours & Travel: See the Real India," *Reality Tours*, accessed February 2, 2010, http://www.realitytoursandtravel.com/.
13 *Ibid.*
14 *Ibid.*

portrayal of the slum as poverty pornography—we are not "dogs" the slum dwellers of India have bellowed—and its romanticization of a way out of the slum—Salman Rushdie has thus dismissed the film as impossibly unreal.[15] Crerar notes that his guide on the Dharavi tour expressed annoyance at the derogatory use of the term "dog": "People were angry with the way they were represented."[16]

Slumdog Millionaire can be read as poverty pornography. It can also be read as a metonym, a way of designating the megacity that is Mumbai. The film depicts the violent nightmare that is Mumbai: the riots of 1992 and 1993 when Hindu nationalist mobs burned Muslims alive in the alleys of Mumbai's slums; and the broken dreams of the migrants who flock to the city but become yet another body in the vast circuits of consumption and capital. Which came first, the fictional and cinematic Mumbai or the real Mumbai of "reality" slum and sightseeing tours? After all, Suketu Mehta's book Maximum City from 2004, which itself redraws the line between fiction and ethnography, is an uncanny shadow history of the real Mumbai.[17] Slumdog Millionaire then is only one of the many fictional technologies through which cities like Mumbai are constituted. The film depicts what can be understood as dhandha—entrepreneurial practice akin to street-level hustling. Everyone is out to make a deal: the entrepreneurs of misery who maim children so that they can beg on the sidewalks of Mumbai; the entrepreneurs of space who replace the slums of Dharavi with sky-high condominiums; and the entrepreneurs of dreams who devise game shows as a world of fantasy for the rich and poor. Slumdog Millionaire itself has come to be implicated in a new round of dhandha: from the "explosion of slum tourism" to the putting up "for sale" of Rubina Ali, one of the film's child actors, by her father.[18] It is this equiva-

15 Alison Flood, "Rushdie Attacks Slumdog Millionaire's 'Impossible' Plot," The Guardian, February 24, 2009, accessed March 15, 2009, http://www. guardian.co.uk/books/2009/feb/24/salman-rushdie-slumdog-millionaire.
16 Crerar, "Mumbai Slum Tour."
17 Suketu Mehta, Maximum City: Bombay Lost and Found (New York: Knopf Books, 2004).

lence of cinema and the megacity/slum that Ashis Nandy
and Mehta highlight in different ways.[19] Nandy argues that
popular cinema in India is the "slum's eye view," with the
slum as an entity that "territorializes the transition from
the village to the city ... from the popular-as-the-folk to
the popular-as-the massified [sic]."[20] In the wake of the
Mumbai killings, Mehta wrote: "Just as cinema is a mass
dream of the audience, Mumbai is a mass dream of the peo-
ples of South Asia."[21] Here, categories of equivalence such
as "popular" or "mass" connect cinema, slum, megacity, and
postcolonial nation. It can be argued that this equivalence
is the condition of subalternity.

The reception of *Slumdog Millionaire* in India was
marked by protests. Pukar, a Mumbai-based experimental
initiative founded by anthropologist Arjun Appadurai and
concerned with urbanization and globalization, presented a
native refusal of the film's violent narrative of slum dhandha. In particular, Pukar took objection to the word "slum"
and sought to reposition Dharavi as a zone of economic enterprise. Here is an excerpt from an opinion-piece by Pukar,
published in the *New York Times* shortly after the release of
Slumdog Millionaire:

> Dharavi is probably the most active and lively part of
> an incredibly industrious city. People have learned
> to respond in creative ways to the indifference of
> the state ... Dharavi is all about such resourceful-
> ness. Over 60 years ago, it started off as a small
> village in the marshlands and grew, with no govern-
> ment support, to become a million-dollar economic
> miracle providing food to Mumbai and exporting

18 Crerar, "Mumbai Slum Tour."
19 See Ashis Nandy, "Indian Popular Cinema as a Slum's Eye View of Politics,"
in *The Secret Politics of Our Desires: Innocence, Culpability, and Indian Popular Cinema*, edited by Ashis Nandy (New Delhi: Palgrave Macmillan, 1999) and
Suketu Mehta, "What They Hate About Mumbai," *New York Times*, November
28, 2008, accessed February 3, 2009, http://www.nytimes.com/2008/11/29/
opinion/29mehta.html?_r=2&em.
20 Nandy, "Indian Popular Cinema as a Slum's Eye View of Politics," 2-3.
21 Mehta, "What They Hate About Mumbai."

crafts and manufactured goods to places as far away as Sweden. No master plan, urban design, zoning ordinance, construction law or expert knowledge can claim any stake in the prosperity of Dharavi ... Dharavi is an economic success story that the world must pay attention to during these times of global depression. Understanding such a place solely by the generic term "slum" ignores its complexity and dynamism.[22]

Pukar's native refusal of *Slumdog Millionaire* is an example of what I term "subaltern urbanism." Writing against apocalyptic and dystopian narratives of the megacity, it seeks to resurrect the subaltern space of the slum as that of a vibrant and entrepreneurial urbanism. In doing so, it confers recognition on urban subalterns and perhaps even on the megacity itself as a subaltern subject. I am interested in this itinerary of recognition and how it shapes the emergence of what Vyjayanthi Rao has described as the "slum as theory"—the "passage from slum as population and terrain" to the slum as a "new territorial principle of order."[23] Indeed, the metonymic slum is central to the formation that I am designating as "subaltern urbanism."

Subaltern Urbanism

It is a hallmark of postcolonial theory that the Gramscian concept of subaltern was taken up by modern Indian historiography, specifically by the group known as the Subaltern Studies Collective.[24] In this appropriation of Gramsci's

22 Mathias Echanove and Rahul Srivastava, "Taking the Slum Out of 'Slumdog,'" *New York Times*, February 21, 2009, A 21.
23 Vyjayanthi Rao, "Slum as Theory: The South/Asian City and Globalization," *International Journal of Urban and Regional Research* 30.1 (2006): 227.
24 See Sumit Sarkar, "The Conditions and Nature of Subaltern Militancy: Bengal from Swadeshi to Non-co-operation, c. 1905–22," in *Subaltern Studies III*, edited by Ranajit Guha (New York: Oxford University Press, 1984) and Gayatri Chakravorty Spivak, "Scattered Speculations on the Subaltern and the Popular," *Postcolonial Studies* 8.4 (2005): 475–486.

"Southern Question," the idea of the subaltern was used to call into question the elitism of historiography.[25, 26] "Emphasizing the fundamental relationships of power, of domination and subordination," the term came to mean a "space of difference."[27] Most famously, in Ranajit Guha's formulation, the subaltern was the "demographic difference between the total Indian population and all those ... described as the 'elite.'"[28] Thus, subalternity came to be seen as the condition of the people, those who did not and could not belong to the elite classes, a "general attribute of subordination."[29] As Spivak notes, in such usage, the term subaltern was closely associated with the idea of the popular.[30] Subaltern politics is thus popular politics and popular culture. Further, in the work of the Subaltern Studies Collective, the agency of change came to be located in this sphere of subaltern politics. In this sense, subalternity became more than the "general attribute of subordination"; it also became a theory of agency, that of the "politics of the people."[31] More recently, Partha Chatterjee has advanced the concept of "political society," a "popular politics" that he distinguishes from "civil society" or the politics of rights-bearing, enfranchised bourgeois citizens.[32] Political society, for Chatterjee, involves claims to habitation and livelihood by "groups of population whose very livelihood or habitation involve violation of the law."[33]

I am interested in this shift: from the subaltern marking the limits of archival recognition to the subaltern as an agent of change. As the subaltern is granted a distinct political identity, so this figure comes to be associated

25 Ranajit Guha, "On Some Aspects of the Historiography of Colonial India," in *Selected Subaltern Studies*, edited by Ranajit Guha and Gayatri Chakravorty Spivak (New York: Oxford University Press, 1988).
26 Sarkar, "The Conditions and Nature of Subaltern Militancy," 273.
27 Spivak, "Scattered Speculations on the Subaltern and the Popular," 476.
28 Guha, "On Some Aspects of the Historiography of Colonial India," 44.
29 *Ibid.* 35.
30 Spivak, "Scattered Speculations on the Subaltern and the Popular," 476.
31 Guha, "On Some Aspects of the Historiography of Colonial India," 40.
32 Partha Chatterjee, *The Politics of the Governed: Reflections on Popular Politics in Most of the World* (New York: Columbia University Press, 2004).
33 *Ibid.* 40.

with distinct territories. One such territory is the slum. It is also in this way that the idea of the subaltern has entered the realm of urban studies, leading to the emergence of a formation that I call "subaltern urbanism." Two themes are prominent in subaltern urbanism: the economies of entre-preneurialism and political agency.

Let us return for a moment to Pukar's native refusal of *Slumdog Millionaire*. Pukar's claim that Dharavi is an entrepreneurial economy is well borne out by the work of various scholars. Jan Nijman, for example, argues that the urban slum is more than a warehousing of surplus labor; it is also a space of "home-based entrepreneurship."[34] It is this economy of entrepreneurialism that is on display in the "reality tours" of Dharavi. This too has a metonymic character, for the slum's entrepreneurialism stands in for a more widespread entrepreneurial spirit—perhaps that of the megacity, perhaps that even of the postcolonial nation. Thus, leading Indian journalist Barkha Dutt writes that *Slumdog Millionaire* is a masterpiece of a movie because it depicts the "the energy, entrepreneurship and imagination of the slum kids." She likens this to "the *jugadu* spirit that is so typical of India."[35]

> Jugadu ... was originally the word for a marvellous invention—a hybrid automotive that welds the body of a jeep with the engine of a water pump and looks like a tractor. Today it has come to be our shorthand for spunkiness—a we-will-get-the-job done [*sic*] attitude no matter how bad the odds are.[36]

In similar fashion, global architect Rem Koolhaas inter-prets the urbanism of Lagos as a "culture of make-do."[37] In his encounter with Lagos, part of the Harvard Project

34 Jan Nijman, "A Study of Space in Mumbai's Slums," *Tijdschrift voor Econo-mische en Sociale Geografie* 101.1 (2010): 13.
35 Barkha Dutt, "Why Isn't India Saying 'Jai Ho?'" *Hindustan Times*, January 31, 2009, accessed March 1, 2009, http://www.hindustantimes.com/Why-isn-t-India- saying-Jai-ho/Article1-372854.aspx.
36 *Ibid.*

on the City, Koolhaas is taken with the inventiveness of its residents as they survive the travails of the megacity. He sees such experimental responses as generating "ingenious, critical alternative systems," a type of "self-organization" creating "intense emancipatory zones."[38] It is not surprising then that Koolhaas draws the following conclusion: "Lagos is not catching up with us. Rather, we may be catching up with Lagos."[39] In this way, the seemingly "alien and distant" megacity becomes the platform for a "neo-organicist" analysis of urbanism.[40, 41] As Gandy has noted, such imaginations turn on the premise of "ontological difference," the African megacity situated outside the currents of world history.[42] There is a lot that can be said about the personage of the star architect and the project of the Third World megacity. But what concerns me here is the emphasis on self-organizing economies of entrepreneurialism and how this leads us to a theory of subaltern urbanism.

Koolhaas, delirious with the power of his own gaze, is easy to dismiss. But subaltern urbanism far exceeds footloose architects looking for new projects of exploration. Koolhaas' ideas are best paired with those of influential global policy guru, Hernando de Soto, whose libertarian optimism presents the Third World slum as a "people's economy" populated by "heroic entrepreneurs."[43] Here, the slum economy is interpreted as a grassroots uprising against state bureaucracy—in other words, a revolution

37 Okwui Enwezor, "Terminal Modernity: Rem Koolhaas' Discourse on Entropy," in *What is OMA: Considering Rem Koolhaas and the Office for Metropolitan Architecture*, edited by Veronique Patteeuw (Rotterdam: NAi Publishers, 2003), 116.
38 Joseph Godlewski, "Alien and Distant: Rem Koolhaas on Film in Lagos, Nigeria," *Traditional Dwellings and Settlements Review* 21.2 (2010): 8-9.
39 Matthew Gandy, "Learning from Lagos," *New Left Review* 33 May/June (2005): 37–53.
40 *Ibid.*
41 Godlewski, "Alien and Distant."
42 Matthew Gandy, "Planning, Anti-planning and the Infrastructure Crisis Facing Metropolitan Lagos," *Urban Studies* 43.2 (2006): 371–96.
43 Hernando De Soto, *The Mystery of Capital: Why Capitalism Triumphs in the West and Fails Everywhere Else* (New York: Basic Books, 2000).

from below. For de Soto, such economies are rich in assets, albeit in the defective form of dead capital. The "mystery of capital" is how such dormant and defective assets can be transformed into liquid capital, thereby unleashing new frontiers of capital accumulation.

There is a striking resemblance between such arguments of economic libertarianism and the utopian schemes of the left. For example, in a sketch of "post-capitalism," geographers J.K. Gibson-Graham celebrate the "exciting proliferation of projects of economic autonomy and experimentation."[44] Making a case for the performing of "new economic worlds," for an "ontology of economic difference," Gibson-Graham showcase "community economies" and urge us as researchers to make them more real, credible, and viable.

Equally important as a theme in subaltern urbanism is the question of political agency. In his widely circulating apocalyptic account of the "planet of slums," Mike Davis expresses anxiety about the political agency of slum dwellers, asking: "To what extent does an informal proletariat possess that most potent of Marxist talismans: 'historical agency?'"[45] Davis argues that "uprooted rural migrants and informal workers have been largely dispossessed of fungible labour-power, or reduced to domestic service in the houses of the rich" and that thus "they have little access to the culture of collective labour or large-scale class struggle."[46] Against such accounts, subaltern urbanism recuperates the figure of the slum dweller as a subject of history.

Take for example the work of Asef Bayat, who argues that, in Third World cities, a "marginalized and deinstitutionalized subaltern" crafts a street politics best understood as "the quiet encroachment of the ordinary."[47] There

44 J.K. Gibson-Graham, "Diverse Economies: Performative Practices for 'Other Worlds," *Progress in Human Geography* 32.5 (2008): 613.
45 Mike Davis, "Planet of Slums: Urban Involution and the Informal Proletariat," *New Left Review* 26 March/April (2004): 28.
46 *Ibid.*

is almost a Wirthian quality to Bayat's analysis, for it is the territory of the restructured Third World city that produces this quiet encroachment. More recently, Bayat has rejected the arguments that link the rise of militant Islamism to the "urban ecology of overcrowded slums in the large cities."[48] The slum, Bayat argues, may not be characterized by radical religiosity, but it does engender a distinctive type of political agency: "informal life." For Bayat, "informal life," typified by "flexibility, pragmatism, negotiation, as well as constant struggle for survival and self-development" is the "habitus of the dispossessed."[49] This idea—of a slum habitus—is a key feature of subaltern urbanism.

In a highly sophisticated account, Solomon Benjamin delineates the differences between three different political arenas: a policy arena penetrated by real estate lobbies and finance capital; a civil society arena that seeks to restrict political activity to those deemed to be "legitimate citizens"; and an arena of "occupancy urbanism" through which the urban poor assert territorial claims, practice vote-bank politics, and penetrate the lower, "porous" reaches of state bureaucracy.[50] Benjamin's analysis is by no means Wirthian. Indeed, his political-economy account of multiple land-tenure regimes firmly grounds the slum in the circuits of finance and real estate capitalism. But in a manner similar to the Subaltern Studies Collective's conceptualization of popular politics, he grants the poor a distinctive form of political agency: occupancy urbanism. Such urbanism for Benjamin is necessarily "subversive," appropriating "real estate surpluses" and possessing a "political consciousness that refuses to be disciplined by NGOs and

47 Asef Bayat, "From 'Dangerous Classes' to 'Quiet Rebels': The Politics of the Urban Subaltern in the Global South," *International Sociology* 15.3 (2000): 533.
48 Asef Bayat, "Radical Religion and the Habitus of the Dispossessed: Does Islamic Militancy Have an Urban Ecology?" *International Journal of Urban and Regional Research* 31.3 (2007): 579–90.
49 *Ibid.* 579.
50 Solomon Benjamin, "Occupancy Urbanism: Radicalizing Politics and Economy Beyond Policy and Programs," *International Journal of Urban and Regional Research* 32.3 (2008): 719–729.

well-meaning progressive activists."[51, 52] In this, Benjamin's analysis bears close resemblance to Chatterjee's conceptualization of "political society" as a space of politics formed out of the governmental administration of populations, but escaping such forms of developmentalism.[53]

I am highly sympathetic to the cause of subaltern urbanism. I see it as an important correction to the silences of urban historiography and theory, the "sanctioned ignorance"—to borrow a phrase from Spivak—that has repeatedly ignored the urbanism that is the life and livelihood of much of the world's humanity.[54] Even Koolhaas' encounter with Lagos, as Godlewski notes, can be seen as a sign of a "growing sense that architectural theory should address global practice rather than singular monuments in the Western world."[55] And it would be naïve to fault subaltern urbanism for the various appropriations of slum entrepreneurialism that today make up an increasingly busy traffic of slum tours, blockbuster films, entrepreneurial NGOs, and globally circulating architects and policy consultants.

In fact, the urgency of such recognition is all around us. Working on the US–Mexico border and tracking the mobile mutations of this militarized urbanism, architect Teddy Cruz searches for "alternative urbanisms of transgression." [56] In border neighborhoods, he finds "a migrant, small scale activism," which he designates as the "informal."[57] These urbanisms, he argues, inhabit space "beyond the property line in the form of non-conforming spatial and entrepreneurial practices."[58] Here is an effort to imagine a "new brand of bottom-up social and economic justice" amidst the

51 Benjamin, "Occupancy Urbanism: Radicalizing Politics and Economy Beyond Policy and Programs," *International Journal of Urban and Regional Research* 32.3 (2008): 719.
52 *Ibid.* 725.
53 Chatterjee, *The Politics of the Governed.*
54 Gayatri Chakravorty Spivak, *A Critique of Postcolonial Reason*, 164.
55 Godlewski, "Alien and Distant," 17.
56 Teddy Cruz, "Levittown Retrofitted: An Urbanism Beyond the Property Line," in *Writing Urbanism: A Design Reader*, edited by Douglas Kelbaugh and Kit Krankel McCullough (New York: Routledge, 2007), 75.
57 *Ibid.*
58 *Ibid.*

brutal subalternity imposed by the global border.[59] How can such a project be denied sympathy?

Working within, rather than against, subaltern urbanism, I hope to pose some critical questions about this project of recognition and its key analytical themes. In doing so, I draw upon Spivak's critique of the itineraries of the subaltern. Writing against those versions of subaltern studies that seek to identify the subaltern as belonging to a subordinate class, as the "demographic difference," Spivak casts doubt on "conscientious ethnography" that hopes to study and represent the interests of the subaltern.[60] This "produced 'transparency,'" she rightly notes, itself "marks the place of 'interest.'"[61] Spivak's work thus challenges us to study how the subaltern is constituted as an object of representation and knowledge—in lieu of the conscientious ethnography that claims to speak for the authentic subaltern. Further, Spivak calls into question the slippage between "subaltern" and "popular" that can be found in the work of the Subaltern Studies Collective and in many renderings of subaltern political agency. In particular, Spivak draws attention to the metonymic character of such frameworks of subalternity:

> Agency presumes collectivity, which is where a group acts by synecdoche: the part that seems to agree is taken to stand for the whole … A performative contradiction connects the metonymy and the synecdoche into agential identity.[62]

With such critiques in mind, I present three challenges to the formation of subaltern urbanism: the first is concerned with the economy of entrepreneurialism, the second with political agency, and the third with archival and ethnographic recognition.

59 Cruz, "Levittown Retrofitted: An Urbanism Beyond the Property Line," 75.
60 Spivak, *A Critique of Postcolonial Reason*, 191.
61 *Ibid*. 265.
62 Spivak, "Scattered Speculations on the Subaltern and the Popular," 480.

Let me return for a moment to the utopian call for post-capitalist worlds by critical scholars like Gibson-Graham. In keeping with the broader formation that is subaltern urbanism, this call pivots on an ontological vision of the people's economy. Gibson-Graham list a set of community economies marked by the register of difference: squatter, slum dweller, landless, informal credit. But it can be argued, as I have in my recent work, *Poverty Capital: Microfinance and the Making of Development*, that these economies are also the active frontiers of contemporary capitalism, the greenfield sites where new forms of accumulation are forged and expanded—in the interstices of the slum, in the circuits of microfinance. It is not surprising that post-capitalist yearnings bear such close resemblance to the frontier ambitions of economic libertarians like Hernando de Soto. De Soto sees in the ecology of the slum a world of dead capital waiting to be turned liquid. He is an important interlocutor in a composition of ideas and practices that I have termed "poverty capital"—the conversion of poverty into capital, the mining of "the fortune at the bottom of the pyramid."[63] The slum, in its territorial density, represents a crucial space for bottom-billion capitalism, one where poor populations can be easily rendered visible for global capital. It is thus that Dharavi, that subaltern site celebrated in the native refusal of *Slumdog Millionaire*, is much more than a self-organizing economy of the people. It is also increasingly visible to global capital as an urban "asset," the "only vast tract of land left that can be made available for fresh construction activities" at the heart of Mumbai.[64, 65] Mukesh Mehta, the architect who is lead-

63 C.K. Prahalad, *The Fortune at the Bottom of the Pyramid: Eradicating Poverty Through Profits* (Cambridge: Wharton School Publishing, 2004).
64 Mark Tutton, "Real Life 'Slumdog' Slum to be Demolished," *CNN*, February 23, 2009, accessed March 1, 2009 http:// edition.cnn.com/2009/TRAVEL/02/23/ dharavi.mumbai.slums/index.html.
65 Singh, "Dharavi Displacement Project," *Civil Society*, August, 2007, accessed January 24, 2009, http://www.civilsocietyonline.com/aug07/aug0712.asp.

ing the controversial Dharavi redevelopment plan, argues that this could be India's Canary Wharf.[66] At the frontiers of redevelopment, the spaces of poverty celebrated by subaltern urbanism are transformed into what I have termed "neoliberal populism," a thorough commodification of community economies.[67]

Similar issues are at stake in the conceptualization of subaltern political agency. While Benjamin does not suggest that the terrain of occupancy urbanism is immune from political machinations, he nevertheless presents it as the subversive politics of the poor, autonomous of developmentalism, state action, and real estate capital. But in the work of Liza Weinstein, land development is also the domain of "development mafias."[68] These "local criminal syndicates, often with global connections," operate in tandem with real estate capital, the state, and the police.[69] This too is an occupancy urbanism—but of the powerful—and it exists in complex interpenetration with the vote-bank politics and territorial claim-making of urban subalterns.

To understand the turn in subaltern studies to the theme of political agency, it is necessary to pay attention to the broader enterprise of postcolonial theory. In an effort to erode the imperialism of knowledge, postcolonial theorists, especially those trained in the *dependista* tradition, have sought to end "epistemic dependency."[70] For Mignolo, this means confronting "colonial difference," that which marks the limits of "theorizing and thinking" and made the world "unthinkable beyond European (and later, North Atlantic) epistemology."[71] As an example of "liberating reason," Mignolo turns to Enrique Dussel's idea of

66 Tutton, "Real Life 'Slumdog' Slum to be Demolished."
67 See Ananya Roy, *Poverty Capital: Microfinance and the Making of Development* (New York: Routledge, 2010).
68 Liza Weinstein, "Mumbai's Development Mafias: Globalization, Organized Crime and Land Development," *International Journal of Urban and Regional Research* 32.1 (2008): 22.
69 *Ibid.*
70 Walter D. Mignolo, "The Geopolitics of Knowledge and the Colonial Difference," *The South Atlantic Quarterly* 101.1 (2002): 85.
71 *Ibid.* 90.

"transmodernity," where "modernity and its denied alterity, its victims, would mutually fulfill each other in a creative process."[72]

Subaltern urbanism, with its emphasis on the subaltern as political agent, is a recuperation of modernity's supplement: the colonized Other. Particularly important here is Vinay K. Gidwani's conceptualization of "subaltern cosmopolitanisms."[73] Writing against a cosmopolitanism that postures "its provincial and prejudiced European origins in the name of the 'universal,'" Gidwani draws attention to "the connections that are possible between the different disenfranchised."[74] Similarly, Colin McFarlane documents the worldliness of slum politics in Mumbai, designating these imaginaries and practices as "slum cosmopolitanism."[75] Such interventions lie at the very heart of postcolonial theory: They disrupt, trouble, and thereby decolonize ideas of modernity and cosmopolitanism. And in doing so, they grant political/postcolonial agency to the subaltern; although as Craig Jeffrey and McFarlane note, "subaltern cosmopolitanism is often contradictory and limited in its political effects."[76]

But what is this postcolonial agency? I am taken with the worldliness of the subaltern, with the unbounding of the global slum, with the new solidarities and horizontalities made possible by such transmodern exchanges. But I am also taken with how the "colonial wound" is the occasion for a host of postcolonial centerings, for violent practices of domination and hegemony.[77] In this transmodernity, postcolonial experiments inaugurated by emergent

72 Enrique Dussel, "Europe, Modernity, and Eurocentrism," *Nepantla* 1.3 (2000): 473.
73 Vinay K. Gidwani, "Subaltern Cosmopolitanism as Politics," *Antipode* 38.1 (2006): 7–21.
74 *Ibid.* 16-18.
75 Colin McFarlane, "Postcolonial Bombay: Decline of a Cosmopolitanism City?" *Environment and Planning D: Society and Space* 26.3 (2007): 480–499.
76 Craig Jeffrey and Colin McFarlane, "Performing Cosmopolitanism," *Environment and Planning D: Society and Space* 26.3 (2008): 420.
77 Walter D. Mignolo, *The Idea of Latin America* (Malden, MA: Blackwell, 2005), 95.

nation-states and their megacities generate and stage global value. Such experiments cannot be read as a reversal of colonial power; instead, they demonstrate the brutal energy of the postcolony. In some of our recent work, Aihwa Ong and I have sought to analyze how such experimental urbanisms produce an interconnected and interreferenced Asia, a complex circuitry and hierarchy of expertise, investment, and development crisscrossing Mumbai, Singapore, Shanghai, Dubai, Manila, and Jakarta.[78] These postcolonial experiments transform the "colonial wound" into the ideology of an ascendant "Asian century," of a history to be dominated by the economic powerhouses of a territory imagined as Asia.

It seems to me that in order to tackle the question of subaltern political agency, it is necessary—as Spivak has noted—to make a distinction between agency and identity.[79] If the subaltern is inscribed as the popular, then it is possible to ascribe an identity to the people's politics. But if we are to return to Guha's original sense of the subaltern as "demographic difference," then this space of subordination cannot be represented by a coherent identity. At best, subaltern politics is a heterogeneous, contradictory, and performative realm of political struggle. It is this performativity that Spivak seeks to capture through a return to the idea of metonymy: "The point is to have access to the situation, the metonym, through a self-synecdoche that can be withdrawn when necessary rather than confused with identity."[80]

Here, the recent work of Craig Jeffrey on *jugaar* is instructive.[81] While subaltern urbanism tends to see jugaar/jugadu as the native make-do attitude of the slum, Jeffrey presents jugaar as a political entrepreneurship that is

78 Ananya Roy and and Aihwa Ong, eds., *Worlding Cities: Asian Experiments and the Art of Being Global* (Oxford: Blackwell, 2011).
79 Spivak, "Scattered Speculations on the Subaltern and the Popular."
80 *Ibid.* 482.
81 See Craig Jeffrey, "Fixing Futures: Educated Unemployment Through a North Indian Lens," *Comparative Studies in Society and History* 51.1 (2009): 182–211.

strategically performed by various social classes. Studying how student hustlers operate within an "informal economy of state practices," Jeffrey shows how young men belonging to a rural middle-class engaged in "shrewd improvisation" to tackle a future of unemployment and economic uncertainty.[82] The importance of Jeffrey's analysis is twofold: firstly, it illustrates how a seemingly subaltern strategy such as jugaar can be applied by various social classes in many different ways (in this case, middle-class students might collude with state officials); and secondly, it highlights the moral ambivalence associated with jugaar and how this ambivalence is negotiated through cultural inventions, all of which draw upon the social basis of class power. As with the case of occupancy urbanism or street politics, jugaar is not the "habitus of the dispossessed," but a flexible strategy instead, wielded differently by different social classes in the context of urban inequality

What then is the subaltern? Where then is the subaltern? In her critique of subaltern studies, Spivak argues that "subalternity is a position without identity."[83] She continues: "Subalternity is where social lines of mobility, being elsewhere, do not permit the formation of a recognisable basis of action."[84] In this sense, the subaltern is neither habitus nor territory and neither politically subversive nor culturally pragmatic. Against ontological and topological readings of the subaltern and building on Spivak's critique, I argue that the subaltern marks the limits of archival and ethnographic recognition. Such an idea returns us to Ranajit Guha's initial interest in challenging the elitism of historiography and Dipesh Chakrabarty's mandate to study the "conditions for knowledge of working-class conditions," with special attention to the "silences" of "ruling class documents."[85, 86] But while Guha, Chakrabarty, and other members of the Subaltern Studies Collective seek to recover the history of subaltern classes, Spivak rejects

82 Jeffrey, "Fixing Futures: Educated Unemployment Through a North Indian Lens," 205-206.
83 Spivak, "Scattered Speculations on the Subaltern and the Popular," 476.
84 *Ibid.*

such an itinerary of recognition. In her work, the subaltern marks the silences of our archives and annals. It is this conceptualization of the subaltern that I believe is most useful to urban studies, for it calls into question the conditions for knowledge through which "slumdog cities" are placed in the world.

Beyond Recognition

In my earlier work, I have argued that the study of the twenty-first century metropolis requires new geographies of theory.[87] Subaltern urbanism is indeed one such approach. It is a vital and even radical challenge to apocalyptic and dystopian narratives of the megacity. However, subaltern urbanism tends to remain bound to the study of spaces of poverty, of essential forms of popular agency, of the habitus of the dispossessed, of the entrepreneurialism of self-organizing economies. I am interested in a set of theoretical projects that disrupt subaltern urbanism and thus break with ontological and topological understandings of subalternity. In the broadest sense, I am interested in the following question: How can we understand the inevitable heterogeneity of Southern urbanism, that which cannot be contained within the familiar metonymic categories of megacity or slum and that which cannot be worlded through the "colonial wound"? With this in mind, I foreground four emergent concepts: periphery, urban informality, zones of exception, and gray spaces. Each concept has a distinctive genealogy and therefore cannot be seen as new or novel. For example, the idea of periphery can be traced to Latin American *dependista* frameworks of world systems and

85 Ranajit Guha, "On Some Aspects of the Historiography of Colonial India," in *Selected Subaltern Studies*, edited by Ranajit Guha and Gayatri Chakravorty Spivak (New York: Oxford University Press, 1988).
86 Dipesh Chakrabarty, "Conditions For Knowledge of Working-class Conditions," in *Selected Subaltern Studies*, edited by Ranajit Guha and Gayatri Chakravorty Spivak (New York: Oxford University Press, 1988), 179.
87 Ananya Roy, "The 21st Century Metropolis: New Geographies of Theory," *Regional Studies* 43.6 (2009): 819–830.

their geographic polarizations. Similarly, the notion of the informal sector was first put forward in the context of East African economies and then traveled to explain forms of deproletarianization and deregulation in many other parts of the world. My claim is not that these concepts are new and therefore worthy of attention. Rather, I am interested in how scholars, working in a variety of urban contexts, are using such concepts to chart new itineraries of research and analysis.

Peripheries

In a recent treatise on city life, AbdouMaliq Simone makes the case for the importance of the periphery in urban life.[88] Simone's concept of the periphery is multivalent. By it, he means cities that have been "at the periphery of urban analysis" and whose urbanism has thereby been ignored.[89] By periphery, he also means a "space in-between ... never really brought fully under the auspices of the logic and development trajectories that characterize a center."[90] It is the "entanglement" of periphery and "possibility" that most interests Simone.[91] On the one hand, the periphery—not unlike the slum—is a space produced through the interventions of humanitarianism, urban restructuring, capital flows, policing, and control. But, on the other hand, the periphery is a "potentially generative space—a source of innovation and adaptation ... potentially destabilizing of the center."[92]

Is the periphery also a place? Simone, following Jacquier, rejects topological meanings of the periphery and instead uses the term to refer to a "range of fractures, discontinuities, or 'hinges' disseminated over urban

88 AbdouMaliq Simone, *City Life from Dakar to Jakarta* (New York: Routledge, 2010).
89 *Ibid*. 14.
90 *Ibid*. 40.
91 *Ibid*. 33.
92 *Ibid*. 40.

territories."[93] But he also identifies the "interstitial zone between urban and rural" as one of several significant peripheries.[94] Similarly, James Holston and Teresa Caldeira, seeking an alternative to the vocabulary of slums, present the autoconstructed peripheries of Brazilian cities as spaces of the invention of citizenship: "Sites of metropolitan innovation," they argue, "often emerge at the very sites of metropolitan degradation."[95] Here, the periphery signifies a relationship of interdependence in an apparatus of domination, but it also refers to a specific topographical location: the peripheral neighborhoods of the urban poor. Similar ideas can be found in the work of the Los Angeles School of Geography, which is concerned with how, in the postmodern metropolis, the hinterlands or periphery now organize evacuated city-cores.[96]

The periphery, even in its topological use, is an important conceptual device to decenter urban analysis. But perhaps most significant is the claim that the periphery is both a space in the making and a form of making theory.[97] Simone, for example, argues that cities at the periphery of urban analysis must be repositioned as an "invented latitude," a "swath of urban life running roughly from Dakar to Jakarta" that has "something to do with each other" and that skirts "the usual obligatory reference to cities of 'the North.'"[98] Here then is an itinerary of recognition that is dramatically different from that of the dominant map of global and world cities. Here then is a cartography of transmodernity. But is the periphery as theory a departure from the slum as theory?

I am convinced that the promise of the concept of periphery lies in its ability to transcend territorial location, to

93 Simone, *City Life from Dakar to Jakarta*, 41.
94 *Ibid.* 45.
95 James Holston and Teresa Caldeira, "Urban Peripheries and the Invention of Citizenship," *Harvard Design Magazine* 28 (2008): 18.
96 Michael Dear and Nicholas Dahman, "Urban Politics and the Los Angeles School of Urbanism," *Urban Affairs Review* 44.2 (2008): 269.
97 Teresa Caldeira, Opening remarks, Peripheries: Decentering Urban Theory conference at the University of California, Berkeley, February 5–7, 2009.
98 Simone, *City Life from Dakar to Jakarta*, 14.

demonstrate various foreclosures that complicate political
agency, and to call into question the conditions for knowledge. Simone, for example, highlights how the periphery
is also a "platform" for "anticipatory urban politics," one
where "peripheral status" can be used as an advantage.[99]
However, this is not a habitus of the dispossessed. Indeed,
Simone insists that the "politics of anticipation is not just
a form of resistance or simply a politics from below" since
"these very anticipations can also be used by more powerful actors and forces."[100] Caldeira goes further, arguing
that poor young men of the periphery use cultural tactics
such as rap to produce a "powerful social critique."[101] But
they also "establish a non-bridgeable and non-negotiable
distance between rich and poor, white and black, the
centre and the periphery, and articulate a position of
enclosure."[102] It is the analysis of such paradoxical forms
of social agency that troubles, disrupts, and expands the
realm of subaltern urbanism.

Urban Informality

Subaltern urbanism functions through slum ontologies.
Such ontological readings of the megacity and its urbanisms have repeatedly invoked the idea of the informal.
Bayat asserts that informal life is the habitus of the
dispossessed.[103] Cruz sees informal habitation at the
global border as an urbanism that transgresses across the
"property line."[104] For de Soto, the informal represents the
grassroots rebellion of the poor against state bureaucracy;
it is a sign of heroic entrepreneurship.[105] Davis states that

99 Simone, *City Life from Dakar to Jakarta*, 62, 28.
100 *Ibid*. 99.
101 Teresa Caldeira, "Worlds Set Apart," *Urban Age*, 2008, accessed June 10,
2010, http://www.urban-age.net/10_cities/08_saoPaulo/_ essays/SA_Cal-
deira.html.
102 *Ibid*.
103 Bayat, "Radical Religion and the Habitus of the Dispossessed."
104 Cruz, "Levittown Retrofitted."
105 De Soto, *The Mystery of Capital*.

"informal survivalism" is "the new primary mode of livelihood in a majority of Third World cities."[106] He thereby
evokes an older usage of the term "informal," that of Keith
Hart, who identified a "world of economic activities outside
the organised labor force" carried out by an "urban sub-
proletariat."[107] In all such frameworks, the informal remains
synonymous with poverty and even marginality. It remains
the territory and habitus of subaltern urbanism.

Against these various interpretations, in my work, I
have argued that informality must be understood as an
idiom of urbanization, a logic through which differential
spatial value is produced and managed.[108] Urban informality then is not restricted to the bounded space of the
slum or deproletarianized/entrepreneurial labor; instead,
it is a mode of the production of space that connects the
seemingly separated geographies of slum and suburb. The
splintering of urbanism does not take place at the fissure
between formality and informality but rather, in fractal
fashion, within the informalized production of space. Informal urbanization is as much the purview of wealthy urban-
ites as it is of slum dwellers. These forms of urban informality—from Delhi's farmhouses and Kolkata's new towns
to Mumbai's shopping malls—are no more legal than the
metonymic slum. But they are expressions of class power
and can therefore command infrastructure, services, and
legitimacy. Most importantly, they come to be designated
as "formal" by the state while other forms of informality
remain criminalized. For example, Weinstein shows how various shopping centers in Mumbai had been "built illegally ...
by the city's largest and most notorious mafia organization,
on land belonging to the state government's public works
department."[109] Or, in the case of Delhi, Asher D. Ghertner

106 Davis, "Planet of Slums," 24.
107 Keith Hart, "Informal Income Opportunities and Urban Employment in
Ghana," Journal of Modern African Studies 11.1 (1973): 61, 68.
108 Ananya Roy and Nezar AlSayyad, Urban Informality: Transnational
Perspectives From the Middle East, Latin America, and South Asia (Lanham:
Lexington Books, 2004).
109 Liza Weinstein, "Mumbai's Development Mafias," 23.

notes that a vast proportion of city land-use violates some planning or building law, such that much of the construction in the city can be viewed as "unauthorized."[110] He poses the vital question of how and why the law has come to designate slums as a "nuisance" and the residents of slums as a "secondary category of citizens," while legitimizing illegal and informal "developments that have the 'world-class' look."[111] Also in Delhi, Gidwani characterizes the proliferation of illegal farmhouses as the "urban conquest of outer Delhi," a process of "unauthorized construction" that involves "cordoning off the few remaining agricultural tracts."[112]

The valorization of elite informalities and the criminalization of subaltern informalities produce an uneven urban geography of spatial value. This, in turn, fuels frontiers of urban development and expansion. Informalized spaces are reclaimed through urban renewal, while formalized spaces accrue value through state-authorized legitimacy. As a concept, urban informality therefore cannot be understood in ontological or topological terms. Instead, it is a heuristic device that uncovers the ever-shifting urban relationship between the legal and illegal, legitimate and illegitimate, authorized and unauthorized. This relationship is both arbitrary and fickle and, yet, it is the site of considerable state power and violence. Urban informality thus makes possible an understanding of how the slum is produced through the governmental administration of a population, as well as how the bourgeois city and its edifices of prosperity are produced through the practices of the state.[113] In this sense, urban informality is a heuristic device that serves to deconstruct the very basis of state legitimacy and its various instruments: maps, surveys, property, zoning, and, most importantly, the law.

110 Asher D. Ghertner, "Analysis of New Legal Discourse Behind Delhi's Slum Demolitions," *Economic and Political Weekly* 43.20 (2008): 66.
111 *Ibid.*
112 Gidwani, "Subaltern Cosmopolitanism as Politics," 12.
113 Chatterjee, *The Politics of the Governed.*

Zones of Exception

The concept of urban informality denotes a shift from slum ontologies to an analysis of sovereign power and its various spatialized negotiations. It also denotes a shift from the territorial imagination of cores and peripheries to the fractal geometries of metropolitan habitation. For a theory of such spatialities, it is necessary to turn to the work of Aihwa Ong. While other theorists have explained the territorial logic of neoliberalism as one of revanchist frontiers, spatial dispossession, or the rescaling of "state spaces," Ong studies "market-driven strategies of spatial fragmentation."[114] She thus traces patterns of "non-contiguous, differently administered spaces of graduated or variegated sovereignty," or zones of exception.[115] From special economic zones to special administrative regions, these zones both fragment and extend the space of the nation state. Such zoning practices have been particularly visible in China, where liberalization has coincided with "zone fever"— the formation of numerous types of zones encompassing economic and technological development zones, high-technology development zones or science parks, bonded zones or free-trade zones, border-region economic-cooperative zones, and state tourist-vacation zones.[116] George Lin thus reports that the thousands of Chinese zones together cover a territory that exceeds the country's total urban built-up area.[117] Indeed, one may ask: In a territory where zones of exception proliferate, what then is the city?

114 See Neil Smith, *The New Urban Frontier: Gentrification and the Revanchist City* (New York: Routledge, 1996); David Harvey, *A Brief History of Neoliberalism* (New York: Oxford University Press, 2005); Neil Brenner, *New State Spaces: Urban Governance and the Rescaling of Statehood* (New York: Oxford University Press, 2004); and Aihwa Ong, *Neoliberalism as Exception: Mutations in Citizenship and Sovereignty* (Durham: Duke University Press, 2006), 7.
115 Aihwa Ong, *Neoliberalism as Exception*, 7.
116 Carolyn Cartier, "Zone Fever, the Arable Land Debate, and Real Estate Speculation: China's Evolving Land Use Regime and Its Geographical Contradictions," *Journal of Contemporary China* 10.28 (2001): 455.
117 George Lin, "The Growth of Chinese Cities in the Era of Volatile Globalization: Dynamics, Challenges, and Opportunities," Paper presented at the Making Global Cities and the World Economic Crisis conference, Shenzhen, January 4–8, 2010.

Ong's work on zones of exception is a crucial counter-point to subaltern urbanism. Instead of slum entrepreneuri-alism, she is concerned with what may be understood as the entrepreneurial state. Ong thus argues: "I maintain that the nation-state—with its supposed monopoly over sovereignty—remains a key institution in structuring spatial order."[118] Such order is produced and managed through "a system of graduated zones."[119] What is crucial about such zones of exception is the "differential deployment of state power": that "populations in different zones are variously subjected to political control and to social regulation by state and non-state agencies."[120] Zones of "superior privileges" coexist and contrast with zones of cheap-labor regimes; transnational zones of investment coexist and contrast with transnational zones of refugee administra-tion; and zones of neoliberal rule coexist and contrast with zones that are exceptions to neoliberalism.[121]

In Ong's theorization, zones of exception are arrange-ments of sovereign power and biopower. She is particularly attentive to the "technologies of subjectivity" and "tech-nologies of subjection" that characterize these systems of zones.[122] Here her work has important connections to the theme of exception present in the work of Giorgio Agamben. For Agamben, the space of exception is a state of emer-gency produced through the sovereign's suspension of the juridical order. It is, as Derek Gregory has noted, a "le-gal—lethal space."[123] But it is also, as Judith Butler points out, a state of "desubjectivation," a space where "certain subjects undergo a suspension of their ontological status as subjects when states of emergency are invoked."[124]

118 Aihwa Ong, *Flexible Citizenship: The Cultural Logics of Transnationality* (Durham: Duke University Press, 1999), 215-217.
119 *Ibid*.
120 *Ibid*.
121 *Ibid*. 219.
122 Aihwa Ong, *Neoliberalism as Exception*, 6.
123 Derek Gregory, "Vanishing Points: Law, Violence, and Exception in the Global War Prison," in *Terror and the Postcolonial: A Concise Companion*, edit-ed by Elleke Boehmer and Stephen Morton (Malden, MA: Blackwell, 2010), 154.
124 Judith Butler, *Precarious Life: The Power of Mourning and Violence* (New York: Verso, 2004), 96, 67.

But states of exception do not stand outside the spaces of metropolitan habitation. Rather, they indicate a specific "legal–lethal" logic of rule that is ever present in the seemingly ordinary spaces of the city. Of the various spatial technologies of exception, Gregory notes:

> The very language of "extraordinary rendition," "ghost prisoners," and "black sites" implies something out of the ordinary, spectral, a twilight zone: a serial space of the exception. But this performative spacing works through the law to annul the law; it is not a "state" of exception that can be counterposed to a rule-governed world of "normal" politics and power.[125]

Writing against Agamben, Ong thus notes that it is not enough to trace the "logic of exception" that is "invoked against the politically excluded" and that is measured in relation to a "universal norm of humanity."[126] In the multiple and differentiated zones of exception that she documents, rule unfolds through freedom, rights-talk, virtue, nationalism, and many other "visions of the good life."[127]

Gray Spaces

In his analysis of the global war prison, Gregory interprets such spaces of exception additionally as "a potential space of political modernity."[128] It is a "profoundly colonial apparatus of power" that gives "form and force" to such spaces.[129] But, as he notes, the "metropolitan preoccupations of Foucault and Agamben more or less erase" this colonial present.[130] The global war prison as a metonym for colonial

125 Gregory, "Vanishing Points," 84.
126 Ong, *Neoliberalism as Exception*, 22-23.
127 *Ibid.*
128 Gregory, "Vanishing Points," 57.
129 *Ibid.*
130 *Ibid.*

violence thus marks the limits of archival and ethnographic recognition. It is also the poignant counterpoint to that other space of political modernity—the popular politics of the subaltern vaunted by Chatterjee.[131]

Gregory's mandate to take up the study of colonialism and its war cultures leads us to the concept of "gray spaces" put forward by Oren Yiftachel. Writing in the context of what he designates as "urban colonialism," Yiftachel describes "gray spaces" as "those positioned between the 'whiteness' of legality/approval/safety, and the 'blackness' of eviction/destruction/death."[132] He notes that these spaces are tolerated and managed, but only "while being encaged within discourses of 'contamination,' 'criminality' and 'public danger' to the desired 'order of things.'"[133] There are important connections between "gray space" and other concepts that I have presented earlier in this article. "Gray spacing" makes evident the flexibility of sovereign power that is at the heart of Ong's analysis of zones of exception. For Yiftachel, such "gray spacing" takes place at the "periphery of peripheries," for example the impoverishment of indigenous Bedouins by an ethnocratic Israeli state.[134] At these colonized margins, Yiftachel argues, "bare life" must be understood "as daily routine, not as exception."[135] And finally, Yiftachel is particularly interested, as I am, in analyzing the manner in which state power formalizes and criminalizes different spatial configurations:

> The understanding of gray space as stretching over the entire spectrum, from powerful developers to landless and homeless "invaders," helps us conceptualize two associated dynamics that we may term here as "whitening" and "blackening." The former

131 Chatterjee, *The Politics of the Governed.*
132 Oren Yiftachel, "Theoretical Notes on 'Gray Cities': The Coming of Urban Apartheid?" *Planning Theory* 8.1 (2009): 88.
133 *Ibid.* 89.
134 Oren Yiftachel, "Critical Theory and Gray Space: Mobilization of the Colonized," *City* 13.2/3 (2009): 247.
135 Oren Yiftachel, "(Un)settling Colonial Presents," *Political Geography* 27.3 (2008): 366.

alludes to the tendency of the system to "launder" gray spaces created "from above" by powerful or favorable interests. The latter denotes the process of "solving" the problem of marginalized gray space by destruction, expulsion or elimination. The state's violent power is put into action, turning gray into black.[136]

Yiftachel's concept of gray spaces both extends and challenges the idea of "colonial difference" and, thus, the epistemic and political location of subalternity. In settings of colonial difference, can the archives and annals yield the voice of the subaltern? Or is such a voice and existence constantly blackened, constantly erased?

Vanishing Points

The elitism of historiography, which sparked the work of the Subaltern Studies Collective, also lurks within the project that is urban studies. Tim Bunnell and Anant Maringanti have recently designated this tendency as "metrocentric-ity."[137] Subaltern urbanism is an important intervention in such conditions for knowledge. It calls into question the "sanctioned ignorance" that attends metrocentricity. Sub-altern urbanism is also a politics of recognition, one that seeks to make visible what McFarlane has called "urban shadows," the "spaces at the edge of urban theory."[138] This is the slum as theory; this is the periphery as theory.

But in this article, I have also called for a disruption of the ontological and topological readings of subalternity, those that celebrate the habitus of "slumdog cities" and assign unique political agency to the mass of urban subal-

136 Yiftachel, "Theoretical Notes on 'Gray Cities,'" 92.
137 See Tim Bunnell and Anant Maringanti "Practising Urban and Regional Research Beyond Metrocentricity," *International Journal of Urban and Regional Research* 34.2 (2010): 415–20.
138 Colin McFarlane, "Urban Shadows: Materiality, the 'Southern City' and Urban Theory," *Geography Compass* 2.2 (2008): 341.

terns. For this I have turned to four emergent concepts—peripheries, urban informality, zones of exception, and gray spaces—that together present the possibility of a different valence of Southern theory. Each of these concepts is, in Mouffe's sense, a "constitutive outside," an outside that by being inside introduces a "radical undecidability" to the analysis of urbanism.[139] Each then is—to borrow a term from both Mouffe and Gregory—a "vanishing point."[140] For Mouffe, a "vanishing point" is "something to which we must constantly refer, but that which can never be reached."[141] This perhaps is the most productive aspect of the analytic concept of subaltern. With this in mind, the four emergent concepts presented here can be read as vanishing points at the limits of itineraries of recognition.

"Slumdog Cities: Rethinking Subaltern Urbanism" was first published in the *International Journal of Urban and Regional Research* 35: 2 (2011): 223–238.

An earlier version of this article was presented as the IJURR lecture at the 2009 meeting of the Association of American Geographers. I wish to thank IJURR, and especially Roger Keil, for the invitation. Gautam Bhan provided valuable research assistance for this project. The IJURR reviewers helped clarify the concept of subaltern urbanism and the purpose of this article.

Bibliography

Bayat, Asef. "Radical Religion and the Habitus of the Dispossessed: Does Islamic Militancy Have an Urban Ecology?" *International Journal of Urban and Regional Research* 31.3 (2007): 579–590.

——. "From 'Dangerous Classes' to 'Quiet Rebels': The Politics of the Urban Subaltern in the Global South." *International Sociology* 15.3 (2000): 533–557.

139 Chantal Mouffe, *The Democratic Paradox*, 12.
140 See Chantal Mouffe, *The Return of the Political* (New York: Verso, 1993) and Gregory, "Vanishing Points."
141 Mouffe, *The Return of the Political*, 85.

Benjamin, Solomon. "Occupancy Urbanism: Radicalizing Politics and Economy Beyond Policy and Programs." *International Journal of Urban and Regional Research* 32.3 (2008): 719–729.

Brenner, Neil. *New State Spaces: Urban Governance and the Rescaling of Statehood*. New York: Oxford University Press, 2004.

Bunnell, Tim and Anant Maringanti. "Practising Urban and Regional Research Beyond Metrocentricity." *International Journal of Urban and Regional Research* 34.2 (2010): 415–20.

Butler, Judith. *Precarious Life: The Power of Mourning and Violence*. New York: Verso, 2004.

Caldeira, Teresa. "Worlds Set Apart." *Urban Age*, 2008. Accessed June 10, 2010. http://www.urban-age.net/10_cities/08_saoPaulo/_ essays/SA_Caldeira.html.

——.Opening remarks. Peripheries: Decentering Urban Theory conference from University of California, Berkeley. 5–7 February, 2009.

Cartier, Carolyn. "Zone Fever, the Arable Land Debate, and Real Estate Speculation: China's Evolving Land Use Regime and Its Geographical Contradictions." *Journal of Contemporary China* 10.28 (2001): 445–469.

Chakrabarty, Dipesh. "Conditions for Knowledge of Working-class Conditions." In *Selected Subaltern Studies*, edited by Ranajit Guha and Gayatri Chakravorty Spivak. New York: Oxford University Press, 1988.

Chatterjee, Partha. *The Politics of the Governed: Reflections on Popular Politics in Most of the World*. New York: Columbia University Press, 2004.

Crerar, Simon. "Mumbai Slum Tour: Why You Should See Dharavi." *Times*, May 13, 2010. Accessed June 10, 2010. http://www.timesonline.co.uk/tol/travel/destinations/india/article7124205.ece.

Cruz, Teddy. "Levittown Retrofitted: An Urbanism Beyond the Property Line." In *Writing Urbanism: A Design Reader*, edited by Douglas Kelbaugh and Kit Krankel McCullough. New York: Routledge, 2007.

Dahman, Nicholas and Michael Dear. "Urban Politics and the Los Angeles School of Urbanism." *Urban Affairs Review* 44.2 (2008): 266–279.

Davis, Mike. "Planet of Slums: Urban Involution and the Informal Proletariat." *New Left Review* 26 March/April, (2004): 5–34.

De Soto, Hernando. *The Mystery of Capital: Why Capitalism Triumphs in the West and Fails Everywhere Else*. New York: Basic Books, 2000.

Dussel, Enrique. "Europe, Modernity, and Eurocentrism." *Nepantla* 1.3 (2000): 465–478.

Dutt, Barkha. "Why Isn't India Saying 'Jai Ho?'" *Hindustan Times*, January 31, 2009. Accessed March 1, 2009. http://www.hindustantimes.com/Why-isn-t-India- saying-Jai-ho/Article1-372854.aspx.

Echanove, Mathias and Rahul Srivastava. "Taking the Slum out of 'Slumdog.'" *New York Times*, February 21, 2009. A 21.

Enwezor, Okwui. "Terminal Modernity: Rem Koolhaas' Discourse on Entropy." In *What is OMA: Considering Rem Koolhaas and the Office for Metropolitan Architecture*, edited by Veronique Patteeuw. Rotterdam: NAi Publishers, 2003.

Flood, Alison. "Rushdie Attacks *Slumdog Millionaire*'s 'Impossible' Plot.'" *The Guardian*, February 24, 2009. Accessed March 15, 2009. http://www.guardian.co.uk/books/2009/feb/24/salman-rushdie-slumdog-millionaire.

Freire-Medeiros, Bianca. "The Favela and Its Touristic Transits." *Geoforum* 40.4 (2009): 580–588.

Gandy, Matthew. "Planning, Anti-planning and the Infrastructure Crisis Facing Metropolitan Lagos." *Urban Studies* 43.2 (2006): 371–396.

——. "Learning from Lagos." *New Left Review* 33 May/June (2005): 37–53.

Ghertner, Asher D. "Analysis of New Legal Discourse Behind Delhi's Slum Demolitions." *Economic and Political Weekly* 43.20 (2008): 57–66.

Gibson-Graham, J.K. "Diverse Economies: Performative Practices for 'Other Worlds.'" *Progress in Human Geography* 32.5 (2008): 613–632.

Gidwani, Vinay K. "Subaltern Cosmopolitanism as Politics." *Antipode* 38.1 (2006): 7–21.

Gilbert, Alan. "The Return of the Slum: Does Language Matter?" *International Journal of Urban and Regional Research* 31.4 (2007): 697–713.

Godlewski, Joseph. "Alien and Distant: Rem Koolhaas on Film in Lagos, Nigeria." *Traditional Dwellings and Settlements Review* 21.2 (2010): 7–20.

Gregory, Derek. "Vanishing Points: Law, Violence, and Exception in the Global War Prison." In *Terror and the Postcolonial: A Concise Companion*, edited by Elleke Boehmer and Stephen Morton. Malden, MA: Blackwell, 2010.

——. "War and Peace." *Transactions of the Institute of British Geographers* 35.2 (2010): 154–186.

Guha, Ranajit. "On Some Aspects of the Historiography of Colonial India." In *Selected Subaltern Studies*, edited by Ranajit Guha and Gayatri Chakravorty Spivak. New York: Oxford University Press, 1988.

Hart, Keith. "Informal Income Opportunities and Urban Employment in Ghana." *Journal of Modern African Studies* 11.1 (1973): 61–89.

Harvey, David. *A Brief History of Neoliberalism*. New York: Oxford University Press, 2005.

Holston, James and Teresa Caldeira. "Urban Peripheries and the Invention of Citizenship." *Harvard Design Magazine* 28 (2008): 19–23.

Jeffrey, Craig and Colin McFarlane. "Performing Cosmopolitanism." *Environment and Planning D: Society and Space* 26.3 (2008): 420–427.

Jeffrey, Craig. "Fixing Futures: Educated Unemployment Through a North Indian lens." *Comparative Studies in Society and History* 51.1 (2009): 182–211.

Lin, George. "The Growth of Chinese Cities in the Era of Volatile Globalization: Dynamics, Challenges, and Opportunities." Paper presented at the Making Global Cities and the World Economic Crisis conference, Shenzhen. January 4–8, 2010.

McFarlane, Colin. "Urban Shadows: Materiality, the 'Southern City' and Urban Theory." *Geography Compass* 2.2 (2008): 340–58.

——. "Postcolonial Bombay: Decline of a Cosmopolitanism City?" *Environment and Planning D: Society and Space* 26.3 (2007): 480–499.

Mehta, Suketu. "What They Hate About Mumbai." *New York Times*, November 28, 2008. Accessed February 3, 2009. http://www.nytimes.com/2008/11/29/opinion/29mehta.html?_r=2&em.

——. *Maximum City: Bombay Lost and Found.* New York: Knopf Books, 2004.

Mignolo, Walter D. *The Idea of Latin America.* Malden, MA: Blackwell, 2005.

——. "The Geopolitics of Knowledge and the Colonial Difference." *The South Atlantic Quarterly* 101.1 (2002): 57–96.

Mouffe, Chantal. *The Democratic Paradox.* New York: Verso, 2002.

——. *The Return of the Political.* New York: Verso, 1993.

Nandy, Ashis. "Indian Popular Cinema As a Slum's Eye View of Politics." In *The Secret Politics of Our Desires: Innocence, Culpability, and Indian Popular Cinema,* edited by Ashis Nandy. New Delhi: Palgrave Macmillan, 1999.

Nijman, Jan. "A Study of Space in Mumbai's Slums." *Tijdschrift voor Economische en Sociale Geografie* 101.1 (2010): 4–17.

Nuttall, Sarah and Achille Mbembe. "A Blasé Attitude: A Response to Michael Watts." *Public Culture* 17.1 (2005), 193–201.

Ong, Aihwa. *Neoliberalism as Exception: Mutations in Citizenship and Sovereignty.* Durham: Duke University Press, 2006.

——. *Flexible Citizenship: The Cultural Logics of Transnationality.* Durham: Duke University Press, 1999.

Prahalad, C.K. *The Fortune at the Bottom of the Pyramid: Eradicating Poverty Through Profits.* Cambridge: Wharton School Publishing, 2004.

Rao, Vyjayanthi. "Slum as Theory: The South/Asian City and Globalization." *International Journal of Urban and Regional Research* 30.1 (2006): 225–232.

"Reality Tours & Travel: See the Real India." Reality Tours. Accessed February 2, 2010. http://www.realitytoursandtravel.com/.

Robinson, Jennifer. "Global and World Cities: A View from off the Map." *International Journal of Urban and Regional Research* 26.3 (2002): 531–54.

Roy, Ananya and Nezar AlSayyad. *Urban Informality: Transnational Perspectives from the Middle East, Latin America, and South Asia.* Lanham: Lexington Books, 2004.

Roy, Ananya. *Poverty Capital: Microfinance and the Making of Development.* New York: Routledge, 2010.

—. "The 21st Century Metropolis: New Geographies of Theory." *Regional Studies* 43.6 (2009): 819–30.

Sarkar, Sumit. "The Conditions and Nature of Subaltern Militancy: Bengal from Swadeshi to Non-co-operation, c. 1905–22." In *Subaltern Studies III*, edited by Ranajit Guha. New York: Oxford University Press, 1984.

Simone, AbdouMaliq. *City Life from Dakar to Jakarta.* New York: Routledge, 2010.

Singh, S. "Dharavi Displacement Project." *Civil Society*, August, 2007. Accessed January 24, 2009. http://www.civil societyonline.com/aug07/aug0712.asp.

Smith, Neil. *The New Urban Frontier: Gentrification and the Revanchist City.* New York: Routledge, 1996.

Spivak, Gayatri Chakravorty. "Scattered Speculations on the Subaltern and the Popular." *Postcolonial Studies* 8.4 (2005): 475–486.

—. *A Critique of Postcolonial Reason: Toward a History of the Vanishing Present.* Cambridge, MA: Harvard University Press, 1999.

—. "Three Women's Texts and a Critique of Imperialism." *Critical Inquiry* 12.1 (1985): 243–261.

Tutton, Mark. "Real Life 'Slumdog' Slum to be Demolished." *CNN*, February 23, 2009. Accessed March 1, 2009. http:// edition.cnn.com/2009/TRAVEL/02/23/dharavi.mumbai.slums/index.html.

Weinstein, Liza. "Mumbai's Development Mafias: Globalization, Organized Crime and Land Development." *International Journal of Urban and Regional Research* 32.1 (2008): 22–39.

Yiftachel, Oren. "Theoretical Notes on 'Gray Cities': The Coming of Urban Apartheid?" *Planning Theory* 8.1 (2009): 88–100.

—. "Critical Theory and Gray Space: Mobilization of the Colonized." *City* 13.2/3 (2009): 246–263.

—. "(Un)settling Colonial Presents." *Political Geography* 27.3 (2008): 365–370.

IMAGE CREDITS

COLOPHON

Editing: Marc Angélil, Rainer Hehl
Art direction: Belgrad
Copy editing: Nathalie Janson

UME teaching team:
Rainer Hehl, Charlotte Malterre-Barthes, Sarah Nichols, Julia Sulzer

Typeface: Executive, Mercury
Paper: Schleipen Bläulich Weiss 70g 2.0 Volume
Printer: Sellier Druck GmbH, Germany

This publication was made possible with the generous support of:

ETH
Eidgenössische Technische Hochschule Zürich
Swiss Federal Institute of Technology Zurich

**(SEC) SINGAPORE-ETH 新加坡－ETH
CENTRE 研究中心**

DARCH
Faculty of Architecture

**(FCL) FUTURE 未来
CITIES 城市
LABORATORY 实验室**

Ruby Press
Schönholzer Str. 13/14
10115 Berlin
Germany

www.angelil.arch.ethz.ch
www.ruby-press.com

Printed in Germany
ISBN 978-3-9813436-6-3